Gender Socialisation among the Tangkhuls

Gender Socialisation among the Tangkhuls

Rv. Khanchuila

GYAN

Published by

Gyan Publishing House
5, Ansari Road
Daryaganj, New Delhi-110002
Phone: 011-47034999, 9811692060
E-mail: books@gyanbooks.com

Distribution Network
gyanbooks.com
India, USA, Canada, UK, Australia, France

ISBN: 978-93-6780-156-7 (HB)
First Published, 2024

Printed at: Gyan Press, Delhi.

Gender Scoialisation among the Tangkhuls

Author: Rv. Khanchuila

Contents

Abstract

Gender studies, though widely recognised in academics and other fields, continue to be a field of study that suggests further scrutiny and efforts. Gender is embedded in every aspect of human lives and each aspect of it needs to be examined to elicit fresh understanding of each part that make the whole mechanism work together. Each pieces of the puzzle placed together gives the portraiture of the complete picture with all shades and colours.

The book is concerned with how gender ideals of masculinity and femininity are embedded in the Tangkhul culture and how this categorisation projects women and men. It deals with the interaction of how these ideals pervade in their lives and how culture shapes these ideals. The context that shapes the ideals is juxtaposed with the categorised ideals that come out in their everyday practices.

The ideals that are entrenched in the society as gender values are examined through the parameter of gender socialisation in this book. It deals with how gender values indorse by the society is passed on to the next generation by examining the process of internalising values by children and the way adults feed the younger ones with stereotyped verbal as well as non-verbal clues.

The changes of the ideals are examined through the agents of socialisation by which the values are passed on. The multi-faceted account of the changing circumstances that shape and reshape gender ideals of the society are underlined vis-à-vis the complex matrix of gender ideals that silhouette the changing times. As such, the book delves into the very fact of performing gender based on biology over the years.

CHAPTER I

Introduction

The first chapter opens with the introduction on overview of the various theories of gender used in anthropology, the statement of problem, pictures of gender in north-east India in general and the existing literature on cultural studies among the Tangkhuls and the sources and methods of data collection.

The present research work is primarily based on data collected through fieldwork, carried out in a village (Somdal Village) located in the western region of Ukhrul District, Manipur. According to the data collected through household census, the village has 470 households with 2334 population (1147 female and 1187 male).

Primary data was collected with the help of household census, observation, interview schedules and case study methods. Interactions between parents and children, actions of parents and children were observed. The period of pregnancy and birth along with three age groups were taken among the children as it marks different levels of socialisation as follows:

(i) **0-5 years**: This is the stage where the children spent most of their time within the home environment.

(ii) **6-12 years:** This is the stage where gendered specific roles and gender segregation becomes more patent which is manifested in their play session and activity performance. It also marks the beginning of learning social status and gender values based on the tradition of the society.

(iii) **13-18 years:** At this stage, children learn to play their role in the social matrix according to the expectation of the society. As they enter a new phase beyond childhood experience, they take on the role of an adult man/woman.

Key informants were also selected from knowledgeable persons in order to procure knowledge of their cultural practices and of the past. The group of aged persons among the key informants other than leaders of political and religious institutions were members of post-Christianity dormitory system (*longshim*). Thus, their inputs to my research work have been fundamental in unravelling vistas of the past.

Informants were selected from three income groups, namely, high, moderate and low to determine the intersection of gender and economy. The revenue, however, is based on the local standard of the village which includes income in cash, agricultural products and handicrafts, converted into cash as per the rate of the village. A total of 372 informants were interviewed and observed for the study.

CHAPTER II

Settings

The second chapter presents the geo-physical picture of Ukhrul district of Manipur where the Tangkhul resides. It also gives an intimate insight into the culture of the tribe with special focus on gender. The descriptive portrait of the structure and practices of their social, economic, political and educational institutions are presented against which background gender analysis on the main theme is discussed.

CHAPTER III

Internalisation of Gender Values

The third chapter opens with the main analysis of the findings. It deals with internalisation of gender values within the family structure by examining changing gendered roles of the members taking two generational studies of the parents and the grandparents. This is followed by discussion on the gendered practices of pregnancy and childbirth and socialisation process at different stages of childhood (0-5 years, 6-12 years and 13-18 years).

The different transitions through which an individual passes during their life, at first sight, seem to be biologically fixed from childhood to adulthood and eventually to death. But the stages of human life course are social as well as biological in nature. They are influenced by biological differences and material circumstances of people's life in a given type of society.

Before a child can accurately label himself or herself as *ngalanao* (girl) or *mayarnao* (boy), they receive a range of clues. For instance, adult men and women handle the infant boy/girl differently, system etic differences in dress and hairstyle and formulate visual clues for an infant in the learning process. This goes on till they are old enough to buy their own clothes or do their own hairstyle. Gender values are tailored to the infant even in the way adult members calm the baby boy by saying that 'Boys do not cry' or console the baby girl, 'Who makes our girl cry?'.

Toys, dresses and other materials which a young child possesses tend to emphasize between male or female attribute. For instance, a boy plays with *kari* (toy vehicles made of wood or purchased from market), *sayur* (toy animals made of clay or wood) while girls are seen with *ngangnanao* (dolls) and *thangthang* (imaginary kitchenware which they make collections out of used bottles and other items). Practically, all children in fact possess and play with gendered toys given to them by parents, relatives and well-wishers. The response to such gender stereotyping also comes from parents and elders who categorically purchased toys for a boy child and a girl child. Even in their treatment towards children, they show stereotypical attitude as girls are not allowed to play with boy's toys and vice versa.

Once gender is "assigned," individuals are bound by social expectations. It is in the practices of everyday life that these expectations are fulfilled and reproduced. For instance, a boy of six years is expected to learn the role of running errands, assist older male, or fetch water. A girl of the same age is expected to learn household chores, learn the basic skill of weaving, and attend to younger children and so on. An adolescent boy, on the other hand, is expected to take on the role of an adult men like repairing works, chop wood, sharpen machete, etc. while an adolescent girl should be able to take on roles like the adult women of the house.

Gendered division of labour is blatantly portrayed among the Tangkhuls which is displayed in socialisation process. Generally, it is observed that parents assign duties and responsibilities to girls which require more time and endurance. Their duties like cleaning, washing, cooking keep them more occupied compared to boys. Assignment of roles to boys could be read from a commonly used saying, *"Mayarnaona khama khangakhai khangachana"*. This literally means that it is natural for boys to bear wounds which typically portray the role of men with strenuous and more perilous tasks.

Some isolated cases were also taken for case studies among families whose gender composition of children consists either only of male or female. Divergence from the typical role performance is observed among these families as gender role segregation are not so rigid and that gendered duties are shared among the siblings.

Individual come to terms with the new roles and physical changes as a boy or a girl adjust with the new phases in their life cycle. In the process, gender values are reinforced by a person's change of status in the society. For instance, the rite of passage among the Tangkhuls varies in different institutions. In their social institution, a boy is not considered an adult to represent the family until he is married. Among the girls, they are only given permanent status only when they become a wife. In their *khanrin* (village political institution), women are not allowed to be members. A boy is inducted into the membership of this institution when they are considered matured enough to participate in the decision-making body, approximately by the age of 18. In economic life, they are counted as adult only when they attain the strength of an adult, that is by the age of 16 and this is applicable for both genders. In the religious life, baptism marks the membership but there is no specific age cut streamlined for such ceremonies.

The outcome of socialisation process is established in the degree of uniformity among the members of a society as they come to share values and attributes. In order to avoid deviation from the norms to ensure social consistency, an adolescent boy or girl among the Tangkhuls, is guided by parents and elders through teachings on the rules of *ngalakhangakhot* (marriage) and *shokhala and vakhalat* (incest). Restrictions are imposed on them to keep away from unhealthy relationship. There are, however, differentials in drawing borders between boys and girls. An adolescent Tangkhul girl is monitored to stay home after dark while permitting boys to go for *meisum* (fireside gathering), an archetypal expression of patriarchy where men are expected to take prerogative in choosing a life partner but not vice versa.

General outline in the socialisation process undeniably shows the immanent interference of patriliny. Parents who believe to give equal treatment to daughters and sons tend to produce different responses when they find themselves in a financial constraint. Manifestation of such responses becomes obvious in their preference of a boy child over a girl child as men are unquestionably the upholder of the family's tradition.

Gender is not a fixed characteristic. It comes out in context of a particular encounter. Gender, as such, change with time, the replication of which could also be traced through gender socialisation. Among the Tangkhuls, social units like *shimkhur* (family), *theisa* (kinship), and *ngalakhangakhot (*marriage), are highly gender institutionalised units where gender values are deeply embedded. Values in other institutions are interwoven with values in these institutions. Analysis of gender roles in the economic institution, for instance is closely linked with gender roles in the family and vice versa. So, changing gender values are studied taking the aspects of the aforesaid institutions.

In the traditional *shimkhur* of the Tangkhuls, decision-making in most cases in the explicit and implicit form shows men as the independent decision-maker who represents the family in the social network. Women were not allowed to participate in decision making. In matters pertaining to their patrilineal system, women were not allowed to take their share except for the share she received at the time of her marriage. The Tangkhuls follow the rule of primogeniture. So, responsibilities rest on the *mayar kharara* (eldest son) to look after the welfare of the aged parents and unmarried siblings. Among the kin members, ties were strengthened by using proper terminologies by each gender and through exchange of goods, labour and help. The kin relations too show that children maintained close relationship with the *varei* (maternal uncle) where the ties were strengthened by frequent visits, love and care from the *varei.* In their *ngalakhangakhot* (marriage), strict rules of clan exogamy were maintained. Violation of which were met with expulsion from the village.

Juxtaposing the traditional practices with the present context, we can ultimately draw a line of difference. Gender role in decision-making today is found to be closely related with economic contribution. For instance, individual's contribution to the family's economy through financial contribution and other means of livelihood shows corresponding impact on their role in decision making. However, the continuum of perpetuity could be located in the core value of patriarchy where women are not allowed to take independent decision without consulting men.

In kinship system, close kinship ties through day to day exchange and visits are now replaced by time to time exchange of material and immaterial tokens as many of the villagers are relocated in different places. Gender marked kinship terminologies too have comparatively lost its vivacity and rigidity. In the past, younger siblings were never allowed to address the eldest brother and sister with their names. They were addressed as '*achon*' (elder sister) and '*amei*' (elder brother). But today, they either address them as *achon* + name or even with their name or pet name. Implementation of marriage rule of exogamy like expulsion from the village today has lost its stringency though such deviations are still grimaced and stigmatised.

The evolving recurrent theme in gender relations today focuses on economic dependency or independence as well. Analysis of this aspect, through the parameter of gender socialisation unveils intersection of gender and economy. The meeting point becomes noticeable when parents are put under a tight financial situation. For instance, more opportunities are open to boys among families of low-income group and some sections of moderate-income group while girls are confined to certain limits as per the capacity of the family as it become a matter of choice. Thus, financial dependency or independence shaped especially by education is predetermined by gender for some families considering the gendered circumscriptions surrounding the economic unit. Such economic response, on the other hand, is provoked by patriliny which is a social foundation of the entire gamut of gender. All these values are, thus, internalised by children through verbal and non-verbal clues given by older members of the society.

CHAPTER IV

Continuity and Change in Gender Socialisation

Continuity and change are examined in the fourth chapter through the agents of socialisation. The socialising agents is discussed under two perspectives; socialisation within the family and outside the family. Continuity and change are determined by tracing the role of socialising agents of the present agents with that of the past that took on its role outlining gender values through its course.

The agents of socialisation are structured group or context within which significant process of socialisation occurs. In the Tangkhul society, the family is the principle socialising agent of the child during infancy. The other influences include the *yarnao* (peers), *worshim* (schools), media, and *dharma* (religion). Continuity and changes in gender socialisation are visible through these agents.

Among the Tangkhuls, gender socialisation takes place within the confines of a nuclear family. The *shimkhur* (family) consist of *ava* (father), *ava* (mother), *naongara* (children), grandparents - *ayi* (grandmother) and *awo* (grandfather), and unmarried siblings of the father - *ani* (aunts) and *avakato* (uncles). The most frequent faces in an infant's life are the *ava*, *ani,* and *ayi*. As soon as the newly born infant is identified through anatomical characteristics, women of the family pamper the infant with gendered oriented behaviour.

As the child learns to imitate gender roles, older siblings play with the younger ones and allocate roles of elders appropriate to one's gender. Play socialisation disappears as children take more substantial role in family. The interference of *shimkhur-chinaongara* (family members) is observed in the child's role learning where adult male members of the family, during this stage, teach young boys in performing their duties, while women take the growing girl child under their supervision. Grandparents take on advisory role as they teach gender appropriate behaviour and expectations of the society through folktales and advices. Analysing the stages of childhood, the mother is the most influential and consistent person in a child's socialisation process as her role shows continuity right from birth till adolescent period.

Outlining the role of today's family as an agent of socialisation, it is found to be a continuation of the role played partly by the family and partly by *longshim* (dormitory) of the past. Values imparted by these agents show perpetuity of preference for a boy child through the years. This is interference of patriliny that placed men on the pedestal as upholders of the family's tradition.

By the age of five, children start to venture beyond their courtyard to play with their neighbourhood friends. They also begin to make friends with other children as they start attending school at this age. This marks the beginning of their socialisation outside the family domain. Different agents like education, religion, peer groups and media, thus, influence the child in the process of socialisation.

In the past, *longshim* functions as the learning centre imparting social, educational, cultural and political values to boys while teaching was limited to social, educational and cultural values for girls. Changes are observed in this light as compared to the modern formal education system where boys and girls are given equal platform for excellence. However, strands of patrilineal continuity are observed in the interference of patrilineal values that finds its symbolic expression in the intersection of economy and gender, where the exigency of economy always comes with gender preference.

Continuity of formal education as an agent of socialisation replicated from *longshim* is perceptible in the association of education and status. In the past, persons who were conversant with customary laws and who shows prowess in war or any skills in economic and other activities were respected. This ideal has now taken the form of educational qualification which tantamount to continuity of roles and functions.

Gender is also embedded in the structure of religion. Among the Tangkhuls, the traditional religion at the village level is a complete portrayal of their patriarchy where women were not allowed to participate in religious rituals. The reality sometimes may be cogently hidden under the heap of an affable social festivities participated by all irrespective of gender. Women, however, undeniably play an important role in rituals at the family level like *chumphu* (festival of opening granary of the newly harvested grains) and *shimshar* (household *Genna*). The portrayal of social locus of the traditional religion is clear with the general outline of men unequivocally occupying the social domain while women's role in rituals is circumscribed only within the family domain.

Analyzing gender in the present structure of their church organisation, gendered perspective cannot be overlooked though men and women participate equally in all religious ceremonies and in the church assembly (which is the decision-making body). In the main religious body, they have pastors (only men), deacons and deaconess (12% women and 87% men), the choir (50% men and 50% women), the youth wings (chairs by men), women wings (which comprises only of married women) and the children department (comprising of all the children of the village).

The present church organisation as a structured group imparting gender values is a continuation of the smaller unit of their old religion-the religious unit of family. Role replication of this agent shows changes in the structure and function which has expanded into a wider scale. For instance, the vigilant role of family in the past as agent of socialisation is limited within the family domain. Church organisation, on the other hand, today brings all members of the village under one single structure and give exposure outside the village through religious activities like conferences and camps.

The term '*yarnao*' is used to designate peer group which, in the past, was basically based on age. The formation of such groups starts by the age of six years. In the past, such groups manifest their solidarity through labour exchange in agriculture activities and feasting/merriment in festivities. The empirical evidence is suggestive of the fact that the structured group of peers as an agent of socialisation have changed in the nature of peer formation. Today, it is not necessarily based on age as there are peer group of schools, church activities, etc. which does not follow a rigid principle of age-based friend circle. Despite the changing nature of this agent, the ideal of *yarnao* as an agent of socialisation is still intact.

Media is totally a new agent which gives access to information beyond the village. This agent of socialisation unquestioningly plays a definitive role in shaping the minds of children in the way it influences their conceptual contour of the embodiment of femininity or masculinity. Though the internalisation of gendered perspective through media is peripheral and that much of it is not in conformity with the intransigent core values of their culture, its influence could not be rout out. Media in the context of the village includes radio, television, newspaper, magazine and social media. Tracing its role in the past, the only window to the outside world was through men who used to go for *khayao* – a labour trip to the plains and occasional barter among neighbouring villages. The traditional exposure was one-sided and the influence was indirect while media today directly influence both men and women.

CHAPTER V

Conclusion

Analysis of the whole findings is discussed in the last chapter giving portraiture of the gender set up that encapsulate the working of gender socialisation of the Tangkhuls. It wraps the study with the findings of how norms and values of gender are passed on to the younger generations and have unwind its course to reach how it stands today.

Intimate insights into the whole matrix of gender socialisation have been discussed through the structure of how gender operates and through the happenings of everyday life. Internalisation of gender values were studied from the perspective of how children learn through verbal and non-verbal clues at different stages of childhood. The study explores gender at three levels:

(i) A child as individual, who internalise her or his identity, and the role of parents and elders, who imbibe gender values through socialisation process.

(ii) The structure of culture that shapes gender relations in the process of socialisation.

(iii) Structured groups as agents, who reinforce gender relations through socialisation process.

Gender values, deeply entrenched in the cultural practices, is reinforced through socialisation. Visualisation of such gendered setup starts involuntarily even before a child is conscious of their own sex. The range of clues, on the other hand, is unwind by people surrounding the little world of the baby with the way they formulate visual clues for an infant in the learning process. Differences in gender attributes stipulate corresponding impact on expectations to women and men. The analysis of socialisation on executing the gendered expectation shows patriarchal values as the recurrent theme. The construction of femininity and masculinity through the prism of socialisation thus, shows hegemony with patriarchy as the core value.

As a person goes through the vicissitudes of life and takes on various fundamental roles, as son or daughter, as mother or father and as grandmother or grandfather, gender socialisation takes on new perspectives though the persistent theme is based on the core value of patriarchy. Learning gender values thus, differs at different stages of a person's life.

The ideological exploration on the attributes of femininity and masculinity projects contrasting gender ideals. The symbolic expression projects men to be more aggressive than women. The standard of expectation thus places men as the protector, which connotes superiority over the ones being protected. Women, on the other hand, co-operates with it in their own subordination.

Juxtaposing the identity of the sexes as women and men within a broad social context of the Tangkhuls, the female identity is aligned to that of men. A woman's status as a daughter or wife is classified with that of men - as daughter of her father and as wife of her husband. Thus, a woman's identity is subsumed with their men which are symbolical representation of their patriliny.

One cannot circumvent or overlook the fusion of the traditional and the cultural imperatives of the outside world which, in other words can be termed as modernity. The substantiation is lucid with generational comparative analysis. Gender roles, for instance, elicit a fresh look in the process of investigation as the gap is perceptible in the way elderly people view younger generations with critical candour on how they perform gendered duties and responsibilities. Thus, gender is not a fixed characteristic. It comes out in context of a particular encounter. Gender, as such, change with time and reproduces itself through gender socialisation.

Against the perspectives on how kin groups maintain solidarity among the older generations through the usage of terminologies, exchange of foods, help, goods, visits, etc., the present symbolic expression of kin solidarity was evaluated to unearth elements of how gender attributes wind its course through the years. Its impact on gender values as a whole in its trajectory is significant in the way the intimacy of the kin group being infringed by relocation of people to different places and the rigid code of gendered terminologies which have lost its vigour. Evaluating the changes through the prism of gender socialisation, the picture of divergence from the old tradition is apparent.

The coalescence of traditional and modern elements of culture is patent. The influx of external elements is apparent in the outlook of the children and the way they adapt to the ways of the outside world. The perpetuity of the traditional values could be seen in the way children dichotomise themselves to the gendered behaviour. These tangible values represented through the symbolic expression thus, foreground the fact that no amount of modernity could dilute their traditional values altogether. These values coexist, replicate or blend together in the process of socialisation.

The unprecedented changes in their cultural practices relating to gender are a response provoked by modernity. These responses are shaped by new circumstances. The vistas of the changing circumstances can be viewed through the spectrum of economic vicissitude through the years. For multiple reasons, traditional subsistence economy, which was the backbone of their economy, could no longer sustain their livelihood.

The economic transformation takes us to the other end of the spectrum and introduces a new status structure with the redefinition of the concept of wealth. This is the juncture, where the status of each sex intersects as individualisation rise its head minimally minimising the shade of gender to certain extent. Money economy, thus, bridged a petite space of gender disparity in decision-making, which however is limited to financial matters as patriarchy transcends all other values that set the centre-stage for gendered practices.

The agents of socialisation play a defining role in bringing about changes as well as in preserving the traditional values. Gender socialisation is juxtaposed against the cultural setup of the Tangkhuls, which poignantly conveys that the same agents of gender socialisation do not play the same role in imparting values through these years.

In the face of the multi-faceted changes that apparently show in their practices, the culture is stringed with rigid patriarchal code which never let their guards down. As such the core values of patriarchy and patriliny are closeted safely in their culture. The way the Tangkhuls organise various institutions, the language they use to describe femininity and masculinity, all point to the fact that gender values of the Tangkhuls are very much intact from external factors. Even the intersection of gender and economy in the present times and the responses of male preference to such circumstances are indicative of their age-old gender values.

According to the findings, it can thus be concluded that gender values have not experienced drastic change. In spite of the continuity of gender values, there is no doubt, that the trends of gender socialisation have changed with changing gender roles. Taking all accounts together, it can be concluded that the predominant cultural circumstances condition gender socialisation of children which cannot tantamount in diluting their core patriarchal or patrilineal values. Through the study, it is obvious that a person's later adult life is always controlled by values that one internalised during childhood. No amount of external forces could dilute the deeply rooted values.

Chapter - I

Introduction

The concept of 'gender' though, arises in the 1970s, is created in varying historical circumstances. Interest in gender asymmetry based on biological differences has been a feature in the discipline of Anthropology since the theory of evolution. The empirical base was laid with the development of ethnography as early as the 1920s when Malinowski (1927), along with detailed descriptions of sexuality, marriage and divisions of labour, stated that emotional development flow from different kinship structures.

Mead (1935) reinforces the base of the concept when she contested the idea of fixed relationship between biological sex and gendered character. Deconstruction of the earlier concept could be read in Beauvoir's (1949) work when she formulated the idea that existence precedes essence; hence one is not born a woman, but becomes one. Distinction between male and female role as the difference of social functions (Parsons and Bales, 1956) was a significant landmark in evolution of the concept. The possibility to explore other areas beyond biological category was further initiated by Schnieder (1968) with his studies on kinship.

The formulation of the concept of 'sex/gender system' (Rupin, 1975) emphasised on the mechanism through which sex, which is understood as some sort of universal biological attribute of the person was transformed into gender, she identified a considerably more flexible and relative, as well as constructed quality. According to this theory, gender as a set of meanings and relationships is related to but not isomorphic with biological sex. Brown and Jordanova (1982) also point out that biological differences do not provide a universal basis for social definitions. What cultures make of sex differences is almost infinitely variable, so that biology cannot assume a determining role.

The widely held concept of "man" or "woman" as stable, ultimately connected to interpretations of biological sex gradually witness a paradigm shift to examination of notions in which gender offers a set of symbols and meanings for interpretation. The reason for this paradigmatic shift is not far to seek with the fact that the inevitable biological difference between the sexes tells nothing about the social significance of that difference. Harris (1993) defines gender as the term to denote the variable emic meanings associated with culturally defined sexual identities as against the etic sexual identity of human beings. As such, gender is a cultural division which in the words of Moore (1994) are fundamentally cultural construction. Gender categories thought to be rooted in biology are also culturally, rather than biologically, constituted that they were ideas framed in particular cultural context which are far more flexible than anyone had previously thought.

The cultural construction of gender takes socially specific norms where the distinction between what is female and what is male is used to structure other cultural contrasts. For instance, a person constructs oneself in relation to the cultural representations of what is male and what is female. As such, 'gender' is a term used to encompass the social expectations associated with femininity and masculinity.

The differentiation of the concept of sex and gender saw burgeoning theories of gender based on universal asymmetries. Rosaldo (1974) with domestic/public domain, Ortner (1974) with nature/culture theory, Meillassoux (1981) notions about universal male superiority and female inferiority through modes of exploitation and domination or Goodale's (1980) concept of pollution where women are considered as polluting which placed them closer to nature.

Though the approach of "universal asymmetry of gender relations" gained momentum during this period, there were, of course, some ethnographers who questioned this approach. Reiter (1975) argues that such notions are imposition of the dichotomised world of the west on others. In the same vein, there are also some ethnographers who, unlike writers who take asymmetrical relations, approach gender as social relationship. They criticize the assumption of universal subordination of women and argued that gender is a social role which holds different values by women and men and in no way these differences imply superiority or inferiority (Leacock 1978, Bell 1983, Sack 1974). Stack (1974) and Weiner (1976) offer new interpretations paying close attention to the voices of women. Faithorn (1976), on the other hand, approaches gender relations analyzing individuals as persons.

The concept of gender relations based on subordination of women were considered as powerful myth about gender relations associated with both the rise of science (Jordanova 1980) and capitalism (Benhabib 1992) in the west. The work of Gillison on indigenous theories of power, and the place of gender relations within it, of the Gimi of Highland New Guinea (Gillison 1993) points out that gender relation differs substantially in different cultures.

A shift from the concept of gender as asymmetrical dichotomies to rethinking of the concept of "self" was formulated by Strathern (1981) who stresses that gender constructs are linked to the concept of self, personhood and autonomy. Any analysis of such concepts necessarily involves some consideration of choice, strategy, moral worth and social value as they relate to the actions of individual social actors.

The theory of 'Gender performativity' put forward by Butler (1990) was also a landmark in the development of the concept according to which the very act of performing gender constitutes who we are. It is real only to the extent of what is performed and that there are no fixed foundations of gender categories.

Later in the 1990s, some (Benhabib 1992, Moore 1994) even argue that the notion of 'sex' or the nature of the biological make-up of men and women is likewise a social construction. So what is recognised as a physically distinct body is not so straightforward a matter as once thought of. The biological 'given' may sometimes conflict with other people's idea about physical reality as some people in Amazonia have no concept of 'body'. A person's capability for reproduction is considered as other worldly source and not a biological matter (Strathern 1992, Overing 1996).

Some others (Croll 2000) argue that ethnographic studies which focus on reproductive or birth culture confirm that sex and gender cannot be distinguished. Likewise Young (2002) puts forward her suggestion that a category of lived body has advantages over a category of gender for feminist and queer theories: (1) no nature-culture distinction is necessary but the body can be described as historically and socially specific; (2) it is not necessary to break out a gendered and "raced" part of identity with this category; (3) differences of sexual desire can be described without recourse to an "inner core" of identity or "sexual orientation." She goes on to argue, however, that it is important to retain gender as an analytical concept.

In the process of seeking explanation for social and cultural configuration, the evolution of the concept shows the multi-faceted phases in the process of locating gender within concrete social situation. Theorising gender at different stages appends the richness of gender studies in locating and understanding gender relations within the historical specific and contextual specifics.

Gender studies, though widely recognised in academics and other fields, continue to be a field of study that suggests further scrutiny and efforts. Gender is embedded in every aspect of human lives and each aspect of it needs to be examined to elicit fresh understanding of each part that makes the whole mechanism work together. Each pieces of the puzzle placed together gives the portraiture of the complete picture with all the shades and colours.

The book is concerned with how gender ideals of masculinity and femininity are embedded in the Tangkhul culture and how this categorisation projects women and men. It deals with the interaction of how these ideals pervade in their lives and how culture shapes these ideals. The context that shapes the ideals is juxtaposed with the categorised ideals that come out in their everyday practices.

The ideals that are ingrained in the society as gender values are examined through the parameter of gender socialisation in this book. It deals with how gender values uphold by the society is passed on to the next generation by examining the process of internalising values by children and the way adults feed the younger ones with stereotyped verbal and non-verbal clues. In the words of Barnard and Spencer, "Socialisation is the process through which people, and especially children, are made to take on the ideas and behaviour appropriate to life in a particular society" (1996: 512). In the words of Wharton (2005), "Gender socialisation is the processes through which individuals take on gendered qualities and characteristics and acquire a sense of self" (2005: 31).

The changes of the ideals are examined through the agents of socialisation by which the values are passed on. The multi-faceted account of the changing circumstances that shape and reshape gender ideals of the society are underlined vis-à-vis the complex matrix of gender ideals that silhouettes the changing times. As such, the book delves into the very fact of performing gender based on biology over the years.

The book seeks to place gender socialisation specifically in the North East Indian tribal context. The existing literature on gender studies in this region could be read in two types of cultural setups; one is the patrilineal (Furer-Haimendorf 1933, Zehol 1998 & 2006, Aier 2008), and the other, is the matrilineal system (Nongbri 1996, Pakyntien 1999, Mukhim 2009). Gender analysis of both patrilineal as well as matrilineal structure depicts hegemonic power relations with male domination and female subordination. However, matriliny is advantages for women (Mukhim 2009). No comprehensive analytical study on gender among the Tangkhul tribe has been done so far. But the existing literatures on different aspects (Hodson 1911, Ruivah 1993, Ruivah and Lurstep 1996, Shimray 2001) coalesce to highlight certain fundamental premises of gender embedded in their culture.

The present research work is primarily based on data collected through fieldwork, carried out in a village (Somdal Village) located in the western region of Ukhrul district, Manipur. According to the data collected through household census, the village has 470 households with 2334 population comprising of 1147 females and 1187 males respectively.

As such this is a qualitative research. As Bodgan and Taylor put it, "Qualitative methodologies refer to research procedures which produce descriptive data: people's own written or spoken words and observable behaviour" (1975:4). In other words, it refers to social research based on field observations analyzed without statistics. This method allows us to see people as they are. The present research is thus a matter of why parents prefer a boy or girl child, and not a question of how many parents prefer a boy or girl child.

Primary data was collected with the help of household census, observation, interview schedules and case study methods. Interactions between parents and children, actions of parents and children were observed. The period of pregnancy and birth along with three age groups were taken among the children as it marks different levels of socialisation as follows:

(i) **0-5 years**: This is the stage where the children spend most of their time within the home environment.

(ii) **6-12 years:** This is the stage where gendered specific roles and gender segregation becomes more patent which is manifested in their play session and activity performance. It also marks the beginning of learning social status and gender values based on the tradition of the society.

(iii) **13-18 years:** At this stage, children learn to play their role in the social matrix according to the expectation of the society. As they enter a new phase beyond childhood experience, they take on the role of an adult man or woman.

Key informants were also selected from knowledgeable persons in order to procure knowledge of their cultural practices over the years. A group of aged persons among the key informants, other than leaders of political and religious institutions, were members of post-Christianity dormitory system (*longshim*). Thus, their inputs to my research work have been fundamental in unraveling vistas of the past practices.

Informants were selected from three income groups, namely, high, moderate and low, to determine the intersection of gender and economy. The revenue, however, is based on the local standard as measured in the village which includes income in cash, agricultural products and handicrafts, converted into cash as per the rate prevailing in the village. A total of 372 informants were interviewed and observed for the study.

This book will analyze how gender values are reproduced through socialisation process and examine how self image of gender is formed. The first chapter opens with the introduction on overview of the various theories of gender used in anthropology, the statement of problem, pictorial images of gender in north-east India in general and the existing literature on cultural studies among the Tangkhuls and the sources, and methods of data collection.

The second chapter presents the geo-physical picture of Ukhrul district of Manipur where the Tangkhul resides. It also gives an intimate insight into the culture of the tribe with special focus on gender. The descriptive portrait of the structure and practices of their social, economic, political and educational institutions are presented against which background gender analysis on the main theme is discussed.

The third chapter opens with the main analysis of the findings. It deals with internalisation of gender values within the family structure by examining changing gendered roles of the members taking two generational studies of the parents and the grandparents. This is followed by discussion on the gendered practices of pregnancy and childbirth, and socialisation process at different stages of childhood (0-5 years, 6-12 years and 13-18 years).

Continuity and change are examined in the fourth chapter through the agents of socialisation. The socialising agents are discussed under two perspectives; socialisation within the family and outside the family. Continuity and change is determined by tracing the role of socialising agents of the present agents with that of the past that took on its role outlining gender values through its course.

Analysis of the whole findings is discussed in the last chapter giving portraiture of the gender setup that encapsulates the working of gender socialisation of the Tangkhuls. It wraps up the study with the findings of how norms and values of gender are passed on to the younger generations and have unwound its course to reach how it stands today.

Chapter - II

Settings

Land

The present study on gender socialisation is discussed as per the findings among the Tangkhul tribe inhabiting in Ukhrul and Kamjong districts of Manipur. The land of the Tangkhuls is bounded by Myanmar in the east, Chandel district in the south, Imphal East district and Senapati District in the west and Nagaland State in the north (www. ukhrul.nic.in).

The people follow a division which is both physical and cultural. It is physical as it follows the direction of four zones as north, east, west and south. It is cultural as the demarcation is based on cultural affinity known as the *Raphei* (north), the *Aze Kamo* (south), the *Zingsho Kamo* (east) and the *Kharao* (west) which according to Luikham (2009) is based on the affinity of their dialect. It should, however, be noted that this division does not follow any system of geographical categorisation under the State administration.

In the process of my intensive fieldwork for this study and for other research projects, I have travelled to many villages of the districts and its topography is wide-ranging. Some places in the eastern region are still well-wooded with dense forests (*kharar-ngahong*). Some areas in the northern side of the Ukhrul district are steep and rugged while some have beautiful landscape with scenic meadows (*khangai*). In the western region, the well-drained rivers are favourable for terraced cultivation (*ngaralui*) which makes it look picturesque during the paddy season. The forest cover of Ukhrul and Kamjong can be seen with different kinds of trees like pine (*ngatang-thing*), oak (shirimthing), walnut (*shirangthing),* etc. The districts come under the tropical rain forest to sub alpine forest (Ruivah 1993).

Stories of my grandfather and elders in the village have it that the land was home to many animals and birds. I, as a child, had the chance of listening to stories of their hunts. The forests are still home to many animals like bears (*singom*), deer (*chao*), monkeys (*nayong*), stag (*sirao*), etc. though the number have declined due to changes in the physical and cultural environment. The stories of fencing the jhum fields from wild animals still fill the mundane talk, which is proof of the rich fauna. The canopy of the forest still shelters many birds like cuckoo (*koktui*), wild pigeon (*nasha*), bulbul (*ramok*), magpie (*meipak*), eagle (*khalang*), etc.

The two districts have a relative climate, and thus, experience a mild summer and a cold winter. The climatic condition is, however, not uniform in all the places. The areas adjoining Imphal valley and Myanmar are comparatively warmer than the rest of the regions. The districts experience sub-tropical climate. The period from June to October is known as *Zur* meaning rainy season. The average rainfall is between 1600 mm to 2100 mm (www.ukhrul.nic.in). The people classify three seasons, viz, *Si* (winter), *Lum* (summer) and *Zur* (monsoon).

The districts are accessible from the State capital through a National Highway 202 (Imphal-Ukhrul) and National Highway 102A (Imphal-Kamjong) from the south-western corner of the district. It is also connected to the neighbouring state of Nagaland from the extreme north of Ukhrul district known as Phek-Jessami road. The areas are also connected to its neighbouring Senapati district from its western parts via Hoomi- Phaibung and Sinakeithei-Khamsom road. Though most of the roads are not pucca road, many detours connect the headquarters to various villages of the district.

Text

With the given physical space of the Tangkhuls, gender operates under the umbrella of the given cultural context. The Tangkhuls are one of the Naga tribes of Manipur (Ruivah 1993:17). The population according to Census 2011 is 1,78,568. They speak Tibeto-Burman language (Hodson 1911, Ruivah 1993). They have a rich variety of languages. A variety of dialects are spoken as many as the Tangkhul villages exist. However, in most cases, dialects under a particular region are to certain extent analogous. At the backdrop of this linguistic diversity, they use '*Tangkhul Tui*' as their common language.

The Field: Somdal Village

An intensive fieldwork was conducted in a village, located in the western side of Ukhrul district. It is situated 21-km away from the district headquarters and 87-km away from the State capital. The village settlement area lies on a slope of the hill overlooking the eastern side. The forest site lies below the settlement area, where shifting cultivation is taken up on five-year rotation basis. The terraced paddy fields are located below the settlement at the foothills near the river that irrigates the fields.

Social Life

Family: In tailing the daily activities and the talks of their lives during the course of my fieldwork, it is apparent that a family for Tangkhul is the core of all their social fabrics. The agrarian economy is based on the reciprocity of labour and produces of their farms, the basis of whose exchange is the family, the smallest unit of their social institution. In a same way, the social matrix is about sharing the bond in times of happiness and sorrow, and that is woven with the family as the nucleus of the social pattern. A sister who has become somebody's wife always comes home in times of trouble to lend a helping hand. A brother who has set up a family of his own never turns a blind eye to his sister and brother.

A Tangkhul family consists of *avā* (father), *ava* (mother), *naongara* (children), *awo-ayi* (grandparents) and *avakato-avakharar* (unmarried brothers of the father) and *ani* (unmarried sisters of the father). The father is known as the *akhava* (head) of the family and he represents the family in all affairs concerning the family. He is the epitome of authority in a family. The embodiment of this value places him as the caretaker of all family affairs; be it decision-making, disposal of family property, or representative of the family in the society. The head of the family thus exercises jurisdiction over all its constituent members of the family. Thus, the structure of the family is patriarchal.

The mother is known as the *akhavaiva* (wife of the *akhava*). She is someone who has entered the threshold of the husband from other family; someone who was daughter of her natal home and her identity is subsumed with that of the husband's family. The picture of a mother is that of a care-giver of family. A mother is looked up by all family members as the pedestal of compassion which is why the home is referred to as the haven of comfort.

Nature of Descent and Inheritance

A young boy, during my fieldwork, politely replied to my queries on his identity that he is the son of Mr. Asan. This evidently illustrates the nature of their patrilineal descent. Generations are linked in genealogical succession through men. Men uphold the name of the family. Women, on the other hand, are not permanent members of her natal home. They change their identity from a daughter to the status of a wife after marriage.

The identity of a woman is subsumed with that of her father or brother if she happens to return home after divorce or other reasons. The children are always affiliated to the husband's family in most cases of marriage within the tribe and a mother, in case of divorce, cannot register her children with her biological family though she could retain custody over the children. There are, however, some exceptional cases of receiving back a woman with her children into her natal community. These are cases of women marrying outside the community. However, the children should be registered into other clan besides her biological clan. This is done so as descent becomes muddled and kin relations are reversed if the children are taken back into the maternal kin.

In the descent structure of the Tangkhuls, the rule of primogeniture is endorsed. The eldest son succeeds his father in the genealogy of succession which is packaged with the ancestral house of the family. He is known as the '*shimkhur khararra*' (head/eldest of the family) which also entitles him with the lion's share of the ancestral property. Other shares are divided among the younger sons. A major share in ancestral properties comes with key responsibility to shoulder further responsibility towards the parents and the younger siblings, until they are settled with their own family.

Within the paradigm of the Tangkhul patriliny, there are certain laws that govern the pattern of inheritance. It is obligatory to understand the concept of property in this context. Among the Tangkhuls, property consists of movable and immovable assets. Movable property consists of possessions like money, ornaments, musical instruments, utensils, agricultural implements, domestic animals or fowls, etc. Immovable property, on the other hand, includes land in the form of settlement site, forest land, cultivable land like terraced fields, etc. It is under the jurisdiction of the parents to bestow the movable properties to whomever they wish to irrespective of gender. Immovable properties unlike the aforesaid, is usually handed down to the male kin and decision on disposal of such property is taken by the lineage male members.

Properties, among the Tangkhuls, are again categorised as ancestral and acquired ones. The ancestral properties are those that are handed down, from generation to generation, through the male kin. The acquired properties are those acquired by an individual during his lifetime. A lion's share of the ancestral property is handed down to the eldest son of the family. A father can, however, bequeaths the acquired property to any of his children including daughters. But, in practice, immovable acquired property usually goes to men of the family as land is never owned in the name of women. If, in any case, a widow without sons owns such property under her name, the property goes to the next male kin of the family after her death. If a man has no male issue, the property goes to his brother's son or to the nearest male kin known as '*shimluikat*', which means customarily authorised person to inherit the property.

The nature of residence is patrilocal. A woman, after marriage, leaves her parental home and enters the threshold of her husband. On the part of the sons, the eldest son takes the parental home while his brothers move out to set up a home of their own (Ruivah 1993). There are, however slight variation among the *Rapheis* regarding this practice. Parents leave the house with the unmarried children after the marriage of the eldest son and set up a new house. This goes on till the youngest son's marriage when they finally move in with the eldest son to retire from all responsibilities (Horam 1977). In the former, the eldest son is responsible for the welfare of his brothers whereas in the latter, the father takes accountability for all his children.

Lineage (*Meiphung*)

Going further from the epicenter of family as the smallest social unit, they have the lineage group known as '*meiphung*' (meaning hearth), a conglomeration of families with a known patrilineal ancestor. Each clan, as such, is sub-divided into many lineage groups.

Clan

The lineage groups form a bigger social unit known as '*shangnao*'. The syllable '*shang*' means group and '*nao*' refers to descendant or children. The term, thus, means association of people based on unilineal descent, consisting of all the descendants in the male-line of common patrilineal ancestor. The clan is a conglomeration of lineage groups known as '*meiphung*'. This lineage is categorised based on the common patrilineal ancestor known to the group. Thus, the fundamental social unit— family, belongs to a *meiphung* and each *meiphung* to the bigger unit – *shangnao*.

Kinship and Marriage

Family is the epicenter of their kinship organisation. All social relations, among the Tangkhuls, establish its root from their kinship structure. Each person maintains relationship with another person according to the expectations and norms of their kin ties. Different terms are used as connotation of their kin ties. The contiguous tie, in their kinship is the kin group known as '*ichichashi*'. The syllable '*ichicha*' means one's own and '*shi*' refers to group. The term covers all agnatic relations on the father's side, covering any generations with whom genealogical generations can be traced through a known ancestor. But, when the genealogy fails to demonstrate its relationship with another, the term '*theisa*' is used to indicate distant kin ties.

The kinship that subsists beyond the aforementioned category is the ties among the clan group known as '*shangnao*'. A well regulated behaviour pattern is maintained within members of the same clan and shares a bond of belonging with one another. In a same way, the populace of a village shares the bond of being inhabitants of the village, which is denoted by the term '*ramnao*'. In fact, a person is identified by his village, among the Tangkhuls, wherever they may be.

To strengthen the kinship ties, there are certain relevant terminologies used to address a person. The usage of the kinship terms denotes the interpersonal relationship of each and every member. These terms have gender specific prefixes.

Avā	:	father
Avākato	:	father's younger brother
Avākharar	:	father's elder brother
Avā + name	:	to all clan's men of the father's generation and maternal aunt's husband
Ava	:	mother
Ava katui	:	mother's younger sister

Ava kharar	:	mother's elder sister
Ava + name	:	to all clan's women of mother's generation and paternal uncle's wife
Amei	:	older brother
Ikato	:	younger brother
Apā	:	older women to younger men
Achon	:	elder sister
Izarva	:	older men to younger women
Ikatuiva	:	older women to younger women
Ani	:	aunty/mother-in-law
Awo	:	uncle/grandfather/father-in-law
Ayi	:	grandmother
Imuilava	:	sister-in-law
Amak	:	brother-in-law (among men)

In their kinship network, the clan is strictly exogamous. Marriage within the clan is taboo and it is forbidden by law of exogamy. The violation of this is known as '*shokhala*', which literally means upside-down. The mother's family line is regarded as the base and foundation of their marriage. A cross-cousin marriage between sister's son and brother's daughter is considered to be the most preferred type known as '*pam*'. However, marriage between parallel cousins is strictly forbidden, that is, between a sister's daughter and brother's son. The violation of this practice is known as '*vakhalat*' ('*va*' means maternal uncle, '*khalat*' means coming back). This way, they maintain a system of kinship where women could receive their nieces into their families as daughter-in-law but not vice versa. From another angle, a girl cannot return to her maternal relations. In this context, even returning to her mother's clan in marriage is considered to meet ill fate.

Monogamy is the standard form of marriage among the people. Polygamy is frowned by the society, and it is regarded as a reproach to peaceful existence of the family. Polyandry, on the other hand, is never mentioned on the lips of the people.

Divorce is very rare among the Tangkhuls. Independent decision by the couple, in case of divorce, finds no legitimacy under the customary laws of the Tangkhuls. The issue can neither be resolved on the ground of mutual agreement as it takes the decision of the whole lineage or clan of both the parties. This kind of rigid customary law avert divorce. But under serious grounds like adultery, divorce is sanctioned. There is no social discrimination in matter of remarriage, but, are sanctioned only after the death of the spouse. The children are, however, affiliated to the kin group of the biological father.

The Annual Social Activities of the Village

The activities of the village populace revolve around the agricultural cycle. Most of their social festivities are related to their agriculture. The two main cultural festivals are discussed as follows:

Luira: It is a seed sowing festival, which falls in the month of February and March, and in the past it normally continues for more than ten days. There is no fixed date for this festival and it is celebrated by each village at their convenient time as per suitable time for seed sowing. This festival holds a propitious aura as the occasion is a ritual to mark the beginning of their agricultural activities, seeking blessings and protection of god for the year's crops.

Certain games and activities are special features of this festivity. Performing *pheichak* (folkdance) and humming *haolaa* (folksongs) are indispensable part of the festival. Games like *khangatuk* (wrestling), *mahar kapai* (high jump), *khayong* (race), etc. are other main features. One prominent characteristic of their fun fare is *khara khangakhun* (tug of war) which is associated with an omen that the rope has to be pulled apart into half by the two groups as a sign of breaking the disturbances for the crops. If it is not broken, it is believed to affect the bounty of their harvest.

The season at this time of the year is marked with the blooms of various fruit trees. Flowers like *mayangtheiwon* (peach), *theikhatheiwon* (plum), *saharwon* (cherries), *kapaiwon* (wild berries), etc. sprouts into full blooms. The people adorn themselves with these flowers during the festival. These flowers thus signify the vibrance of their *Luira* celebration, the exuberance of which is their wish for the joy of a bountiful harvest.

Risit Phanit

Risit phanit, like the seed sowing festival, is a traditional festival related to the agricultural cycle of the people. It is celebrated after the transplantation of paddy saplings ends in their terraced paddy fields which fall in the month of July. This festival is thus celebrated only in some villages where terraced paddy cultivation is practiced. The word *'Risit'* comes from the syllable *'ri'* meaning medicinal and *'sit'* meaning sliced, the literal meaning of which may be interpreted as slicing off insecticides into the fields. They sliced the peel of a variety of medicinal bitter grapefruit known as *'singomthei'* and placed it on the bamboo net at water outlets of the fields. This way the indigenous insecticide is dispensed through the water outlets.

So, this festival is an occasion to celebrate the end of their strenuous working period of transplantation as well as a ritual to seek protection for the crops. One remarkable event of this festival is the lighting up of resonated pines at night in front of their courtyard. This signifies the passage of their agricultural cycle from tiring and hectic period to more leisurely interlude of their agricultural routine.

The advent of Christianity eclipses many cultural festivals, the discontinuation of which may be attributed to their response to change. One important reason is the change of belief system where early missionaries of the new faith made them believe that everything related to the old religion is taboo for the new faith. This way all rituals and ceremonies related to festivals like *kashong kahao* (rituals to protect the transplanted crop), *kaita mawonzai* (rituals after weeding for protection of crops from natural calamities), *tharshat* (rituals before harvest for bountiful harvest), etc., were abandoned and the beliefs of the people were diverted to the new ways.

A significant factor for discontinuation of various festivals is change of lifestyle. With the advent of education and other economic trade, people engage more on other activities besides agriculture. For instance, traditional festival like *yarra phanit*, festivals of youth, lost its relevance today as youths could not spare their time for such celebration in their quest to keep pace with the changing times.

While some traditions of the Tangkhul discontinued, some replicated in other forms. Some other traditions were modified with a new twist whereas some religious festivals have been introduced with the advent of Christianity. This is true with the traditional festivals too. This change may be seen in *'Chumphu Phanit'*, a festival of opening the granary for the newly harvested grains. Instead of long celebrations with many rituals and ceremonies, they now pray over the grains one Sunday morning in the Church. Christmas and New Year celebrations are new additions of festivities that came along with the advent of Christianity.

Festivities, for the Tangkhul as also with the other tribes, depict an egalitarian picture with people participating in all merriment. This was, however, not the state of affairs in the past as the rituals and ceremonies were archetypically patriarchal in many aspects. Women were not allowed to participate in the ritual of the festival performed at village level. They were not allowed to partake in the feast prepared with the sacrificial meat of *luira* festival. However, women would join in all merriment of the festivities like games, singing folksongs or dancing to the beat of their folk dances. In contrary to what was practised in the past, there are no such restrictions today.

Besides festivals, there are certain social activities which are very characteristic of the Tangkhul social institution.

***Yarthot*:** The syllable '*yar*' refers to group of the same age group, and '*thot*' means generation. The term thus refers to a social group of the same age group, formed primarily for economic purpose, which however are clustered under social group as the bond of friendship extends beyond economic operations. This group, which is based mostly on age and gender, works together on rotational basis. The group will work, for instance, in a person's field for a day and continue with another's field on the next day till they finish the turn of the whole member of the group. It is based on age as the capacity of performance differs with age. It is based on sex as there exist gendered division of labour that the nature of women's work and men's work varies markedly. However, there are also instances where men and women form this group work together irrespective of the work nature.

Meisum: The term literally means fireside gathering; '*mei*' meaning fire and '*sum*' meaning gathering or grouping. The term derives from the practice of youth gathering, which usually takes place by the fireside of their kitchen to spend their leisure time together at night as people in the village go about with their work during the day. Boys take the initiative for such gatherings. They visit the girl's house in groups or may be done individually. In the past, *meisum* took place in the girl's dormitory where they gather to sing folksongs and sharing folktales.

Economy

In Tangkhul village, one would hardly find a working adult at home during the day. My fieldwork is undertaken either in the morning or at night, except for the interview with the elderly or interaction with the small kids. I never get to interview an adult, who could perform agricultural activities during the day as agriculture is the mainstay of their economy. Rice is the stable food of the Tangkhuls.

The agriculture cycle begins as soon as their New Year celebration is over. At places where (*ahanglui*) jhum field are practiced, men start to clear the forest right after the festival. In Somdal village where the fieldwork for this study was conducted, they follow a cycle of five years for that particular plot. So, the work of clearing the forest is lighter and easier in the subsequent years. After few weeks of drying off the branches, they burn the leaves and twigs while women clear the surroundings grasses with spade to prevent the fire from spreading to the adjacent forest. The unburned big branches and twigs are then cleared by women using *kharphang* (hoes) while men terraced the steep slopes with the big branches to prevent soil erosion.

Luira festival inaugurates plantation of the year as they sow their seeds in their shifting cultivation sites. Some villages, especially of the eastern and southern region practice paddy plantation in their jhum field. But the village under the present study utilizes the forest for vegetable plantation, particularly potato farming locally known as *mayangpailui*. This crop is supplemented by vegetables like *kopi* (cabbage), *linglonthei* (beans), *kasathei* (chilly pepper), *karopthei* (cucumber), *kayanghan* (mustard), etc.

People wait for the early spring shower to till their terraced paddy fields at the foothills. With the onset of rain, the terraced are tilled, sometimes manually by women using spades or by men using their bullocks. This process of tilling their dry terraced paddy fields is known as *akanglui kahui*. This process is followed by fencing and tilling of their seed bed for paddy saplings known as *mathalui*. Grasses and twigs are cleared at the small plot which is usually near the vicinity of the terraced paddy fields for easy ferrying of saplings to the fields during their transplantation period. It is then burnt after a week to prevent the patch from weeds. The sapling belt is tilled by women while men fenced them to prevent it from cattle.

The jhum fields in the forest areas are ready to tend for weeding by the time they finish their works in the paddy fields. While women take the responsibility of weeding the crops, men see to it that the surrounding trees are properly pruned so that the crops get proper sunlight. In some case, weeding of the forest farm is done once, while others do it twice according to the density of the weeds. And then, they wait for the crops to mature.

The middle part of May marks the beginning of their busy season in the terraced paddy fields. The villagers, in groups, march to the fields for fishing at their *rayilui* (wet terraced paddy field integrated with pisci-culture). The fishing is undertaken in order to prepare the field for paddy transplantation. The practice is known as *luiphat,* which literally means drying off water from the paddy fields. As the water in the fields runs dry, women perform the fishing using *kanta* (small fishing net rounded with bamboo). They tie a basket, known as *shikhang*, on their waist while they go about fishing. Men, on the other hand, plough the fields when the fishing is done. *Luiphat*, a kind of preparatory agricultural activity for the terraced fields, is stringed with social significance as it is woven with meanings of kin ties. Relatives are invited for fishing which is a form of acknowledging and renewing their ties.

The whole process of transplantation starts with ploughing and culminates with paddy plantation, a period that witnesses the most hectic activity for the cultivators of the village. Women are seen every morning rushing to their paddy fields with basketful of food supplies and agricultural implements, while men are seen carrying spade on their shoulder. The sight of their movement to and from the fields is nothing less of merriment, despite the tiring and busy life. They move together in groups talking and chatting in warmth bonhomie, which is indeed a form of bonding among the people.

The sight of their duties during this busy season is marked with gendered division of labour. Women clear the sides of the fields with spade while men plaster the *tankui* (terraced edge) with the sticky mud from the fields for water retention, and plough the fields. Men perform the task of levelling using spade as women busy themselves with *matha khamao* (collecting the paddy saplings from the bed). Small girls and boys ferry the bundled saplings to the field in their carry baskets.

After thoroughly ploughing the field, the water level is left very low for transplantation. Women in groups croon and transplant the paddy, while small girls distribute around a handful of sapling bundles. Sometimes, men are also seen with women in transplanting activities, but the usual practice of this job is meant for women. After this activity, the busiest season comes to an end with men sealing off the water outlets (*ratak*) of the fields at proper level.

People, who were mostly seen flocking downwards to the terraced fields, would now move uphill for the shifting cultivation with their basket on their backs. The end of June sets the beginning of their harvest in their forest farm. It is time for harvesting vegetable crops like potato and beans, which they are popularly known for. Women usually do the harvesting while men help them in ferrying the products home.

The villagers enjoy a short leisurely week in the early part of July as they celebrate *Risit* festival. This period does not last long for they have to turn their attention to weed the paddy fields. As women weeds the fields manually, men would clear the sides of the paddy fields using a sharp flat bamboo stick known as *thingkhai*. They would also clear the surroundings of the field. Weeding is usually done twice. With smoke emanating from the small huts of the paddy fields, the scenic beauty of the fields during this season is accentuated by the lush green crops.

The end of September marks the beginning of harvest season. The picture of activities in the paddy fields clearly portrays the gendered division of labour. Men are seen, as they begin their harvest, preparing the platform with thick layers of haystack where they spread a big sheet of sack cloth on top to gather the paddy grains. This patch is known as *tankui*. As women harvest the crop, young girls bring the stalks in bundles to the *tankui,* where men beat them off on a flat stone, separating the grain and the stalk. Women position themselves in a row to harvest the crop using sickle (*changkui*), and from time to time, one would see their hands going up to their fish basket stringed to their waist to put the fishes they catch as they move along. By the end of the day, they would pack up the grains in sacks and ferry them to the bullock cart or vehicle, to be transported to their granary in the village. After a paddy harvest, it is followed by another harvest of late crops in their forest farm like *maranthei* (soyabean), *theirathei* (grey speckled beans), among others, and this marks the end of their agricultural cycle.

The technique of their agriculture is rather traditional, despite technological developments in other aspects of their life. Their tools and implements are simple. All agricultural activities are performed manually. People do not go for modern fertilizers and pesticides, except in emergency situation like severe infestation of pest. They consider the use of such modern chemicals as detrimental to the soil for the next season. However, new varieties of grains and pulses have been introduced.

Animal Husbandry

Animal husbandry is closely associated with the life of the people. The practice of rearing animals serves different purposes. The primary reason may be attributed to the diet of people which consists of meat with other vegetarian food. Any celebration, festivity or feast, is not complete without a butchery of their domestic animals. This has its roots in the rituals and ceremonies of the past that entail sacrifices of domestic animals and fowls. In the past, any form of imposing fine was demanded in the form of domestic animals. So, domesticated animals or fowls were most valued wealth and persons with these assets were considered wealthy.

In the present times, rearing of such animals or fowls show participation of both genders. Tending cattle (buffalo - *silui,* cow - *simuk*) are considered as the duty of men, whereas domestic animals (dog - *fa*, pig - *hok*) and fowls (*har*) are attended mostly by women. But in cases of commercialising these livestock, both men and women equally participate in rearing these livestock and some make their livelihood out of these economic unit.

Handicraft

A group of elderly men sitting at the courtyard with their sharp elongated knife trimming bamboo sticks is a regular sight in Tangkhul villages. Men, during the off-season from agricultural activities, keep themselves busy on wood works, out of which they make household implements, weaving implements and agricultural tools. This is indicative of the skills of the people with indigenous handicrafts and it is a significant part of their economic sustenance.

Pangthem, a local parlance for handicraft among the Tangkhul, incorporates crafts like bamboo craft, woodcraft and stone works. The word '*pangthem*' – '*pang*' means hand and '*them*' indicates skill. All these activities are considered as masculine trade. Out of bamboo, many functional items in their kitchen like *machikhong* (a block cut out from the bamboo stem as salt container), *peirin* (long flat spatula), *luk* (basket for storage), *yamkok* (tightly woven rounded plate for husking foodgrains), *phungshar* (suspended mantle over the fireplace for drying food items) to name a few, are made of. Women in the past used *tabu* (a well-knit woven basket with a lid) to store clothes. Weaving implement like *rathing* (a long stick) and fishing aids like *shikhang* (fish basket) and *kanta* (fishing basket) are made out of bamboo.

An outside influence is though very apparent in design of their woodcrafts; people still use their own products. They depend on the craftsmanship of their own people and one would hardly find woodcrafts imported from outside. Their woodcraft includes furniture and utensil items. A widely used crafts are *chaoki* (chair), *pamkhong* (low stool), *kapei* (spoons), *naitilung* (small mortar and pestle to make food paste), and *shimkhur-sikui* (giant mortar and pestle for pounding paddy grains). Weaving implements like *rapamthing* (stand to weave the cloth), *kapem* (a long flat weaving implement), *raluithing* (a smooth thick and rounded stick to roll the woven part in rotation), among others are smoothly carved out from wood. Handles of their tools and implements like *khainao* (small kife), *khaipak* (big dao), *yotpak* (spade), *karphang* (hoe), sickle (*changkui*) and *ngaha* (axe) are also made out of wood.

Weaving

It is a common sight to notice women sitting on their front porch engrossed in weaving. While one weaves, another would be seen rolling the thread while some other would be busy with the spinner. As they are busy with their weaving materials, they would also be seen busy in good banter. This is a way of bonding among women. Of the small-scale industries, weaving is one of the most important trades among the Tangkhuls which is considered a feminine trade. The early writings on the tribe by Hodson thus describes "Six Tangkhul villages, Ukhrul, Toloi,* Naimu,* Sandang,* Tuinem,* Phadang,* are specially engaged in the industry of cloth weaving". (Hodson 1974:45).

(* The names of these villages are presently known in order of sequence as Talui, Ngainga, Somdal, Phalee, Teinem).

An important supplementary economic activity is weaving apart from agriculture. It serves as one main source of income for a family. Out of this industry, women produce their ethnic wears like *kachon* (shawl), *kashan* (lower garment), *paitu* (bag), necktie, and other ethnic products like cushion cover, file cover, purse, etc.

Women take up this economic activity whenever they are free from their agricultural activities and household chores. This profession demands great patience and concentration as it is time consuming task as engraving the intricate designs are woven manually. The threads used today for weaving is of a very fine and tiny texture, and it takes almost a month for a professional weaver to complete a finished cloth. For some women, this is an important source to support their children for education.

Employment in Public and Private Sector

Interaction with children, during my fieldwork, shed lights on the people's concept of livelihood. In some way or the other, people find all possible means to stratify their survival. This is evident in the way they express their desire to lead a life with salaried job when they grow up. Their dream is but an indicator of their concept on this aspect of the economy. The introduction of modern education system giving rise to employment in public and private sector emerges as another important unit of their economy. Almost all households of the village have a person gainfully employed either in public or private sector. Many families have been relocated to different parts of the country for this purpose.

Trade

An old man, a key informant for my study, narrated a story about the trade system of the past which he witnessed as a small boy. He went along with his father to a place called *paosaitru,* which is an hour walking distance from the village, to trade their products with that of the traders from the northern Tangkhuls. According to his account, people of the neighbouring villages come to the spot to exchange their goods which however took place once in a while. His account speaks of the past barter system.

The present trade in the village shows a mosaic of diverse trading system. A row of shops is located in the middle of the village selling products from outside and in each and every locality; there are small shops all around selling basic necessities for people in the neighbourhood. It is a common sight everyday to see local taxis packed with passengers to and from the district headquarters who are mostly shopkeepers, suppliers, or local traders. The local agricultural produces like potatoes, plums, cabbage to name a few go to the district headquarters during the harvest season. This trade witnesses participation of both men and women.

Carpentry

In a quite surrounding of the village, the sound of sawing or hammering will be heard somewhere in some corner or the other of the village. The carpenters are busy constructing houses or making furniture. This occupation is exclusively considered as men's trade, though not all men are tailored for this work as it requires skill to partake. The common types of houses in the village are wooden houses except for few concrete buildings. The furniture they use are mostly wooden ones. All these are constructed and made by the local carpenters. It is a lucrative trade according to village economic measurement.

Blacksmithy

The art of blacksmithy locally known as *mari kashem* is an age-old industry. The art of making tools and implements is entirely manual, which requires a lot of energy owing to its strenuous nature. This is another occupation considered as men's trade. The local blacksmiths make agricultural tools and household implements for which the iron is imported from outside the village. The villagers go to the blacksmith to mend their tools and also to sharpen it. The onset of agriculture season, especially before the sowing and transplantation, are the busiest time for the blacksmith. Economically, it is an insignificant trade that has a low returns. However, the industry still survives to meet the needs of the villagers.

Food Processing

The food processing unit is of recent origin. The locally available fruits and food items were never put to process until the recent time. A considerable quantity of excess fruits was seen falling off on the ground, while some were plucked and gifted to neighbours and relatives alike. In certain occasions, food items were stored for family consumption only. In present days, no fruits or vegetables are left wasted with the emerging prospect of revenue from the sales of processed fruits and foods. Now, a variety of local items are processed in the form of pickles and dry fruits, and they are found to have high demand in markets at the district headquarters and the state capital. However, it should be noted that this is in context of the village under study, and it may not be the case with other villages of the Tangkhuls.

Most of the women are engaged in food processing unit. The role of men could be seen in gathering of fruits from the forest. The whole process of making and manufacturing these products are performed by women. It is a time-consuming task as processing is done manually. But since the ingredients are available in their own garden and that the fruits are collected from the forest for free, this activity serves as a profitable unit of economy.

The nature of these economic activities shows gendered division of labour in every aspect of their economy. Women are assigned with activities that are time consuming. Men, on the other hand, take on with the tasks which require strength and strenuous energy. For instance, women goes with an activity of transplantation which involves physically bending and concentrating on the lines and spaces between the saplings, while men use the spade and till the soil in a field. This confirms the concept that men consume more quantity of food than women.

The gendered domain of women and men is another feature in their economic activities. In general, women are assigned with works which could be performed within the home domain. Instances of these activities are weaving, food processing, etc. This is also evident in the economic aspect of livestock rearing in which women tend the domestic fowls and animals. Men, on the other hand, are engaged with activity which is outside the home domain. It is apparently seen with men tending to their cattle and occupying with carpentry. The economic aspect of their culture depicts gendered division and it is indicative of the whole gender relations of their culture.

Political Organisation

The Tangkhuls follow monarchical form of government headed by the village chief known as *awunga*. The seat of chieftainship is hereditary and his office is permanent in nature. He summons and presides over a meeting of the *hangva* (village authority). He is the guardian of his subjects and all responsibilities of care and protection rest on his shoulders. In the pre-Christian period, he functions as the religious head. Every village festival and feast was opened with a ceremony by the *awunga*. In the context of the village, there was a village priest - *sharwo* known as *shimthui luithui khamiya,* who assisted the chief on occasions related to their agriculture activities.

In their political setup, the chief is assisted by the members of village authority known as *hangva*. In the past, members to the village authority were represented by the clan heads and elders, who are well versed with the customary laws. The *hangva* headed by the *awunga*, constitutes the decision making body in their political structure. They formulate policies of war, peace, economy, social activities, among others. It was the highest body in temporal affairs of the village.

In the past, there was no written constitution and the foundation to rule was strictly based on tradition, usages, customs and conventions. In all these, it also entailed religious sanctions. In case of any feuds between parties where decision cannot be reached, they were made to take an oath or swearing in the name of god. For instance, when a feud within the clan could not be resolved by the clan, they would resort to oath taking where the decision was left to the supernatural being for its own course of action.

The village, in the past days, was an independent unit. During this time, there were constant feuds among the villages. The reason were mostly violation of inter-village laws, divorce without proper cause, taking of heads by fraud, etc. In the accounts of Hutton (1930), Furer-haimendorf (1933) and Mills (1935), it is mentioned as head hunting. However, according to the data of the present research, strangers were never beheaded without a good cause. All these feuds would sometime lead to war between the villages, and the heads of an enemy brought home during this time were considered as trophies. A person who could take and bring more heads was honoured as a hero. He would be known as *khamarappa* or *raivat kathema*. However, it was a taboo to harm women and children during such times. It was also forbidden for man to touch a woman for certain period of time until the war is over.

In war time, women play an important role in dispute resolution. A group of women would interfere during such conflict and they were known as the *phukreila*. It refers to women who were married outside and against which her natal villagers were in dispute. *Phukreila* acted as the peacemaker during these periods through dialogue for peaceful settlement. For their noble role for peace and harmony, they were placed on higher pedestal than the common women in the society.

The advent of the British in this hill district witnessed tremendous changes in the political institution of the people. The most outstanding change is the end of inter-village feuds. The advent of British brought about a situation for peaceful co-existence among the people. The powers of the village chief and members of the village authorities were put under check and balance by the British rulers. The situation brought about by the British allows the people to know and understand each other better. This paved way for free movement among the villages. Conflicts which could not be resolved at the village level were brought to the British rulers.

The post-independence period of the country further brought about changes in the political institution of the Tangkhuls. The villages in the hill district, which functioned as independent units, were merged with the Indian union. Gradually, a new form of administration was introduced in many villages to bring about a more democratic form of local governance. A new system in the form of chairmanship, in which the person is elected by the people for tenure of five-year, has been introduced in various villages. The chairman, along with his *hangva* who are also nominated by the people, runs the local administration. However, the chairman oversees the village administration in consultation with the headman and has to take the latter's consent in all matters of the administrative affairs.

The chairman and village authority members are elected by members of the village assembly. The franchise to the membership in the village assembly is based on gender and age. Only male members, who are considered matured enough to partake in decision making, are enrolled for membership in the village assembly. From time immemorial, women are not allowed to participate in the village assembly. They are not entitled to take membership in this political institution, except for one village (*Ringui*) which had in recent years passed a resolution to induct women as members to the village assembly. However, at the time of collecting data for this work, that change did not happened yet. The structure in decision making body of the village political institution is strictly patriarchal.

Religion

The traditional religion of the people was based on the belief in the existence of a supreme god known as '*ameowa*', who is considered to be the creator and benefactor to all his creations. They also believed in the existence of a benevolent and a malevolent spirit. They believed, for instance, in the existence of household spirit - a benevolent spirit, who guards and protects each and every member of the family. On the other hand, they also believed in the existence of a malevolent spirit known as '*chipee*', who inflicts harm to the people. For instance, there are certain places in the village considered to be haunted known as '*ngalei kharar apam*', where the malevolent spirits dwell, and people would avoid going to such places. To propitiate the anger of such spirits, they performed sacrifices and rituals to ward-off bad fortune.

They also had strong belief in omens. To predict the outcome in whatever they do, certain divinations were performed such as *harra khayang* (egg divination), *kapa kapang* (bamboo divination), *harkho khayang* (cock divination), etc.

The traditional religion placed the village chief as the head of their religious institution. He would inaugurate all festivities of the village and performed necessary rituals and ceremonies of the village community among the Tangkhuls. In certain rituals, he was assisted by the *shimthui luithui khamiya* – a priest. At the clan level, the clan head performed the ceremonies. At the family level, the head of the family dons the mantle of a priest. Thus, they confined their religious duties within their own domain.

The head of the family, the clan heads or the village chief are men whose seats are hereditary. The father hands over the headship along with the duties and responsibilities to a son. Though men acted as the priest at the clan or the village level, the role of women is indispensable at the family level at certain religious *genna* and festivals. The role of women, during the celebration of *chumphu* festival, is remarkable. The wife of the household (*akhavaiva*) performed the rituals of opening the festival by taking out basketful of newly harvested grains from the granary. However, such roles are confined only within the family domain and no women could execute it beyond their households.

With the expansion of the British rule over the north-eastern region of India, the Christian missionaries too expanded their work. There were gradually many foreign Christian missionary organisations working among the people in north-east India. Rev. William Pettigrew came to Imphal in 1894 for the purpose of spreading the gospel. His movement was, however banned by the then State Superintendent, Major Maxwell for fear of any provocations to the orthodox Hindus in the Imphal valley. He, thus, moved out from the valley and proceeded towards Ukhrul in the year 1896 and began his mission work among the Tangkhuls (Shimray 2001).

In order to convince the people that he had come for the service of the people, he established a school in 1896. But, the response of the native people was very poor. To persuade and attract more people, he set up a dispensary attached to his residence. He treated many people and cure their ailments and diseases using modern medicines. Comparing their ethno-medicines with that of the modern medications that the missionary administered, people were amazed with the results. Many people flocked in to his dispensary, which became a means of winning the hearts of the local people.

It was not until 1901 that converts were made (*ibid* 2001). Tracing the history of the village, the seed of Christianity was sown in 1909 by the first convert of the village, Rs. Ruichumhao. There was no regular worship place in the initial years. They gather at different places as per their convenience. In the later years that followed, people started construction of the church and a regular place of worship was set up in 1923 (History: Somdal Baptist Church, Centenary Publications, 2009).

The present religious institution of the people functions as one important institution in the lives of the people. Under the umbrella of this institution, there are appointed functionaries to look after its affairs. The church pastor is head of the religious institution. He is assisted by an associate pastor. Men are normally a preferred choice in the appointment of church pastors, who may or may not be members of the local church. They have specific terms of service.

The board of deacons and deaconesses are chosen from among the members of the church to assist the pastor in running the institution. The gender representation, however, is not balanced and may always vary. Of the 15 – 17 deacons, there may be two or three women representation according to the capacity of the church. The institution also has office staff comprising clerk or secretary, peon, technician, etc., and men are always appointed for these positions.

The church has choir members and musicians, and they are supervised by a choir director. They are chosen from members of the church. Membership to the church choir is equally represented based on gender. The directors of this group, as per records in the church history, are predominantly men. However, there is no fixed gender rule on the post of director or that of the musicians. Other functionaries of the church are the stewards with equal gender representation.

There are different wings in the church based on gender and age. The women society is exclusively for women members of the church. The youth society is a unit of the church, and its membership is based on age, gender and marital status. Membership of women in the Christian Youth Society is determined by marriage, as they are inducted as members of women society after marriage. Men, on the other hand, continue to be members of the youth society so long as they could be of service to the society. Children department is another unit which functions for the welfare of the children members of the church.

In contrast to the past religion, the contemporary religious institution has written code of conduct, based on the Bible. Members of the church are bounded by the Biblical doctrine. All religious ways and teachings are also based on this theology.

Health

The modern medical practices and medicines were unknown and unheard of before the advent of Christian missionary. Every sickness, ailment and disease of the people was treated with their ethno-medicinal and medical practices. The medical practices of the people were interlinked with their belief system in many ways. For instance, they believed that the sickness was inflicted by a malevolent spirit and the response is seen in their sacrifices and rituals to propitiate the spirit. In those days, they depend solely on ethno-medicine which is mostly herbal treatment. '*Khanong*', the then medical practitioner, treats and diagnoses people suffering from different ailments. *Khanong* could either be women or men, and they are normally believed to possess healing nature.

With the advent of modern medical practices, the concept of people on health has changed considerably. They no longer depend on the treatment of *khanong* which, however, should be noted that their role for certain ailments have not been ruled out altogether. They are still visited and called home for massage, fracture and treatment of minor ailments.

Education

The concept of education without script would sound bizarre to some as reading and writing has become indispensable in modern education. The Tangkhuls, before the advent of Christian missionary, had no schools or colleges. They never had history written down in the form of books nor do they keep records in black and white. However, tracing the life and culture of those days, the apparatus at which education functions leaving its cultural practices intact through the ages, appeared to be well formulated. Though the impression of education without the script appears to be obscure, education functioned smoothly with oral tradition. These include laws, ethics, customs, values, art, handicraft, etc. All these were carried out in an institutionalised centre of learning known as *Longshim* (dormitories).

The centres of learning were set up separately for boys and girls. The dormitory of the girls was known as the *ngalalong,* where only unmarried girls were given membership to this institution. The dormitory of boys was known as the *mayarlong* and they were admitted by the age of 12 or 13. No such formalities were however observed for girls, and they could join the centre even at a much younger age. Different values were imparted separately to girls and boys.

The dormitory as an educational institution was hosted by certain families in the village. The village chief, in consultation with his council, chose the households based on criteria that could give protection and comforts to the wards of the dormitories. It was indeed considered an honour to be a host of this institution. The head of the family thus acts as the guardian for the wards of the dormitory. He saw to it that all the members of the dormitory were well protected and that they had all they need.

In the teaching-learning process, the dormitory system had no employed teachers. The most skilled and disciplined senior member of the dormitory was entrusted with the duty as a prefect. This person looked after the welfare of the members and took the responsibility to teach values through oral tradition, and also impart vocational skills relevant in their survival.

Those hands-on training on various skills in the dormitories were markedly gendered. Girls were taught to learn the skill of weaving, spinning yarn out of cotton and the art of dipping the yarn in flour water before weaving, stitching, and so on. Boys, on the other hand, were trained with the art of handicrafts on bamboo, wood, etc. The duties and responsibilities appropriate to each gender were also tutored in the institution. Certain values considered feminine and masculine were imparted in these institutions. The values of femininity like hospitality, patience, politeness, were taught to the young inmates of girls' dormitory. Masculine values like decisive usage of statement, authoritative character, and protective character, among others were taught to the inmates of the boys' dormitory. In addition, teachings on customary laws and practices were also part of the dormitory syllabus.

With the advent of Christian missionaries, schools were established and children were then primarily forced to attend these institutions. The new system of education infringed on the smooth functioning of the traditional education institutions. In the old system, the children helped their parents as and learnt various activities with their peers too during the day. In the evening, they go to their respective dormitories and spent their time learning values till they retired to their respective dormitories. Those practices could not go in tune with the new system as children had to attend schools during the day and had to perform their assignments at home.

The aforementioned factor, along with the conversion of religion into a new faith, made it more difficult for the dormitory system to survive. The Christian missionary focussed more on the new system of education and was not in favour of the old practice. However, the advent of Christianity and the introduction of schools did not totally demolish the dormitory system in the early post-Christianity era. It continued for some years, but with marked changes in the practices of the old system. As per the data of the village, they were taught to learn Christian hymns and Bible stories instead of the old syllabus.

The introduction of formal education to the hill district could be traced to the time when the first missionary set afoot in 1896. A primary school was set up that year recruiting 30 students from different villages. In the following years, the poor response from the people prompted the then Superintendent Major Maxwell in passsing orders to the village chiefs to send children from their respective villages.

A temporary school was set up in the village in 1919 and was attended only by boys selected from different clans. Gradually, the school was upgraded and girls too were enrolled in the formal education system. At the present times, there are three schools in the village. Today, every children of the village, except for those who are differently-abled and who could not afford to go outside the village for special education, are enrolled in the institutions irrespective of gender.

In every aspect of the Tangkhul society, there are norms attached to what constitute femininity and masculinity. Within the paradigm of the Tangkhul culture as discussed above, the following chapters will analyse gender socialisation from different perspectives.

Chapter - III

Internalisation of Gender Values

Every society has its own traditions, and perpetuates itself by passing its values and rules along to its younger generation. Some refer to this process as socialisation. Herskovits (1955) proposes "*enculturation*" as alternative term. As these terms suggest, it is a process of inculcating as well as internalising the cultural values to an individual in order to create uniformity among the members of a society as they come to share values and attitudes. In addition to being told about gender, the child actively observes 'significant' others and draws conclusion about the rules governing gender.

The Tangkhul society, though controlled by strict traditional customary laws, enjoys an affable social environment. Men and women, irrespective of age, work together and eat together without segregation among them. They mix freely in all social and festive activities like dancing, singing, etc. Yet, both sexes are expected to maintain strict moral standard and decency. Since they embrace the philosophy of collective good and mutual benefit for all, they believe in the virtue that the welfare of one is for the whole group and ignorance of one will affect the interest and benefit of the entire group.

The broad picture of social festivities, and the way women and men enjoy the light moment in their mundane lives at face value is, however, deceptive. The value of patriarchy among the Tangkhul society permeates in all aspects of their culture. Women are always expected to be submissive while taking cognizance of the cardinal importance of men's power and authority. To understand the internalisation of gender values, we need to have perspective on the family structure, the base and the fundamental unit of social institution.

Family structure

The father is the head of the family. He represents the family in all matters. The family, in the context of the eldest son, consists of father, mother, children, unmarried siblings and grandparents, whereas younger brothers set up their own family after marriage. The family of the younger son, thus, consists of father, mother and children. Daughters, on the other hand, leave the house after marriage.

Family is the fundamental social unit among the Tangkhuls. A person's identity starts from home. His identity in the society is given through his family. For instance, he cannot be a member of the *meiphung* (lineage), *shangnao* (clan) or *ramnao* (villagers) if he is not a member of the family. They share a close relationship within members of the family.

The title of the head of family is entwined with responsibility towards members of the family. A father sees to it that his family members are well protected. The eldest son as an heir to the title and property of his father is bound with responsibility to look after the welfare of his aged parents and his siblings. The same reason is responsible for the brothers to look after the welfare of the married sisters and their children's welfare.

Gendered division of roles within the family is apparent among the Tangkhuls. The father is the authoritarian head of the family while management of the family is associated with the mother. In the same way, other members of the family have their own role as daughter, son, grandmother, grandfather, aunt and uncle.

There is, however, intersection of gender roles with age, in that changes are observed in gender roles among different generations. The feminine role of a mother taken by a mother-in-law shows a shade of variance with that of the daughter-in-law. This was unveiled during my interview with the elderly ladies who are mostly in octogenarian and nonagenarian category, which was juxtaposed with that of the younger generations.

Case 1**:** ***Shin****, a school teacher, is a busy mother. She was seldom at home in the morning before school, and even during the afternoon after school, as any other teachers are expected to. It took me quite some time to catch up with her, as my informant, for an audience.*

When I sat down with her, I was really surprised to learn that she lived her mundane life like any other women in the village. Her morning was spent running to the rice mills, searching for labours in the paddy fields and paying off wages for the works done. In the afternoon, she would hurry off to the jhum or busy tending the livestock at home. That was the reason why I could never catch up with her in my desired time.

On a fine Sunday morning after the Church service, she related how she had been bearing for years a burden as a working mother. Shin is the breadwinner of the family. She spent a junk of her salary on educating her four children. Likewise, she had to pay electric bill, local subscriptions and contributions, taxes and saw to it that there were adequate provisions for the family. For instance, if there was a need for labour in the fields, she would seek out and hire them. With a heavy sigh, she narrated that it took whatever resources she had as a teacher and a mother to keep the family running, and had little time and space for herself.

A comparative study was taken up with the role of her mother-in-law—an octogenarian, to examine the marked changes between her time and now, I sat and interacted with her at length during the day, and thereafter for few more days. The old woman, on the other hand, depended on her husband to buy all the essential items from outside which, however, were of not much required during her days as they depended largely on their own produces. Her husband provided the basic necessities like clothes, household needs among other things, with the meagre earnings from his labour.

The old woman also took me back to their times, as she related, how she had lived a life as a young mother. She was a hardworking woman, who would always make sure that her barn never runs dry and ensured that nobody goes hungry in the family. In those days, the people were never bothered of converting the value of goods into currency as the economy was solely confined in the village. There was no practice of buying and selling in the village. Any excesses from their fields were shared amongst the relatives, neighbours and friends.

As we resumed our interaction another afternoon, she narrated a touching experience of her helplessness as a mother. Her husband did not allow their daughters, the eldest two among five children, to continue their studies after the tenth grade, citing financial constraints. It was a disappointing period for her to watch her daughters so dejected and heartbroken. In such situation, she was but helpless and shed sad tears for many days. There was no other means for her but to console her daughters—saying better things would come their way.

Case 2: *My fieldwork, besides gathering data for the study, was a rewarding experience, especially with the aged elders with whom I chatted with throughout the day as they are at home, retired from the agricultural activities in the field. We shared jokes along the discussion. In the village, most of the elderly people were available during the day as they usually did not work beyond their courtyard. Though at times I found them restless and they would always try engaging in whatever way they could inside the premises.*

The elderly women had had many experiences and anecdotes to share with—for instance, a differing conflict with the younger generations. An 80 years old woman, **Athing**, *has been an early riser all her life. The story of contrasting lifestyle between her and the younger generations came to the fore, when I mentioned that I had to take leave for my lunch. It really took her by surprise when I talked about lunch in the middle of the day.*

After lunch, when I got back to her, she had snacks in hand for her tea while she gave me that mischievous look and punched in a comment, "This is why I faced a sulky daughter-in-law every morning". She confessed that she could not tolerate women who wake up when the sun is high up in the sky. As she recalled her days as a young mother, she spoke of how she would perform all her heavy household chores like fetching water from the pond and pounding rice grains, before any members of the family rise from their beds.

To lighten up her worries and complaints, I told her that the rice mill of the village would be locked before sunrise and that she need not run to the far-away pond as the water supply comes right to the house. On this, the old woman could not but agree more with me. However, she admitted her praise for her daughter-in-law with the exception of the latter being a late riser. She would often wake her up before sunrise, and that she did, with a worry that she may not be able to finish her morning chores. Unlike her days, the daughter-in-law would no more pound the paddy grains in the backyard, but take it to the mill. She would help the children with their studies as she cooks, and fetches water any time in the day as it is supplied right to the house.

The case studies show a vivid picture of the changing role and responsibility of women through the years. Women have stepped into roles which were hitherto out of bound for them. With the changing roles come different responsibilities in a new package which the women would never shoulder in the past.

The changing role is also true of men in the family. The grandfather witnesses his son taking up roles which he would never perform during his time. In determining changing role of men, case study was conducted on decision making, one of the outstanding features of the Tangkhul patriarchy. This case study is incorporated as it represents a classic example of changes observed in the core structure of patriarchy.

Case 3: Angam, *an 84 years old man, was a rigid patriarch, who always stood his ground when it comes to decision-making. In my research work, he was one of the key informants and well-versed with the customary laws and practices.*

He was among the first settlers of a locality in the village— the settlement of which was developed in the early post-independence period.

The data of this case study came up incidentally while gathering information among the younger generations. The case mentioned herein as part of their story was later confirmed with Angam's wife, who otherwise would not have revealed on her own accord.

Angam owned a large area in the new settlement site. As the duty and responsibility of being the eldest son in the family, he parted a plot of land to his brother Ayo. He took the decision and acted upon it in conformity with a custom that it was his bounded duty to see to the welfare of his younger siblings. His wife, on the other hand was not pleased with the decision and was further enraged when he disregarded her suggestion on the choice of location and area. Her disapproval on the matter was that they have three sons, who would later need their own plot of land after their marriage. She felt that Angam was far too generous with his brother, and inconsiderate of their sons' future.

The matter was discussed upon between the spouses for few days. But, it soon turned unpleasant as the husband vent his anger and slapped his wife. He reprimanded her saying that it his discretion, and she had no say in the matter concerning the family's immovable property.

On being enquired of how she dealt with the situation and land issue, she narrated the story in her best joviality. She refused to cook and stayed in bed while skipping three consecutive meals. On the issue of land, she never took the matter up with her husband again.

A comparative study on patriarchy and decision making was taken up with that of Angam's son, Asing. After a series of interactions, the issue of decision-making on the occasion of his son's marriage cropped up.

Asing had a serious discussion with his wife with regard to all aspects of their son's marriage. A section of elders from their Meiphung put up a proposal that they should prepare and arrange a generous presentation for all their **Yorla** *(married women of the family) worth Rs 1000 in addition to the mandatory share of meat. Any eligible member of Yorla in a family, according to the customary practice, is given a gift during a marriage.*

The proposal of Meiphung elders became an issue, which led to serious discussion between the husband and wife. They had differing opinions. While Asing felt that the proposal should be accordingly met, but his wife thought it otherwise. The wife, considering the number of 31 members of Yorla, opined that they should not exceed the amount of Rs 500 for each member.

The discussion turned into an argument. They stood their own ground on the matter for many days. The argument, which was initially between the couples, eventually took the participation of all family members during their mealtime. Some members insisted that they should go ahead with the lineage decision based on the virtue that the groom was the eldest son, while other members argued that their financial position should be taken into consideration as life will go on.

After serious and lengthy deliberation, Asing came to a decision and fixed the rate at Rs 1000 for the immediate kin, Rs 800 for the immediate family kin of the groom's generation and Rs 500 for the distant Yorla. To this, the wife had to give in and agreed to the proposition— considering the pressure from the kin members.

Taking the consensus decision of the family, Asing put up the proposal in the Meiphung meeting and accordingly, obtained their approval.

Changes observed in the roles of gender may be attributed to the responses of people in adapting to the changing needs. A woman, who merely execute as per the decision of the husband in the past, now openly shares her views. Similarly, a man discusses the family issues with his wife. However, women are not expected to be assertive while expressing their opinions. They are expected to state their opinions as recommendation. Moreover, though women's participation is observed in decision-making, yet ultimately the line is drawn and she cannot take independent decision without consulting her husband. Thus, women are marginalised to sharing opinions while the final consent is always given by men.

The importance of currency is deeply entrenched in the economy of the people today, unlike the past when wealth was measured on a different scale. Properties are now calculated in terms of market value. In order to find out decision-making of family in the financial matters, the data were collected on the financial management based on gender.

Table 10. Financial Management of Women and Men

Category	Financial support by women	Financial support by men	Joint management by men and women
Low Income Group	—	—	100%
Moderate Income Group	31%	38%	31%
High Income Group	40%	50%	10%

Source: Fieldwork.

In the low-income group category, men and women jointly manage the financial matters of the family which they earned through wage labour, carpentry, weaving, handicraft, etc. The moderate-income groups are mostly employed in public and private sectors. Among these families, women are seen almost at par with men in the financial status where 31 percent is managed by women as against a slightly higher 38 percent managed by men, while 31 percent are jointly managed by both the genders. The high-income groups portray a different picture where men managed 50 percent as against 40 percent by women. The remaining 10 percent are jointly managed by both genders.

In coalescing all the income groups to highlight the overall image of the society on financial management, it is observed that 22 percent are financially managed by women. While 50 percent are jointly managed by men and women, 28 percent are financially dependent on men for their sustenance.

Alongside the changing gender roles in decision-making and financial management, gender role in their domestic responsibilities and childcare too witness certain changes that may be attributed to alteration of roles in other aspects of their economy. In my quest to find out what could really be a distinctive feature of change in matters regarding domestic responsibilities and childcare, a series of interviews taken were revised, and further, intensive analysis was made to extract more data from it. Following are case studies worth considering.

Case 4: *In the village life of the Tangkhuls, no woman was exempted from domestic responsibilities and duties of childcare under normal circumstances. Anyone trying to flout the norm attracts criticism from relatives, neighbours and society. However, the facets of change become apparent after comparative studies made between the older and younger generations.*

In the present time, no woman is confined within the four walls of village. Some have to go to the nearby towns for some reason or the other, while leaving their family for days together at times. Like any other women of the village, ***Azing*** *ensured her source of income through weaving, apart from selling her agricultural produces. But, unlike the produces from the field that could be sold within the village, she had to sell her handloom products in the town or elsewhere when there are no buyers in the village. Whenever her weaving products are ready, she would then visit the district headquarters. During her absence, she would entrust the responsibilities to her daughter who had come of age to perform the chores including fetching water, cleaning, doing the dishes, attending to the younger siblings, etc. But as the girl had not yet picked up a culinary skill, the father in the house would be the one to cook for the children— a task which he would never have touched upon when a wife is around.*

In the present context, the case as this looks quite normal. During the absence of their wives at home, there are instances of men taking care on domestic fronts.

Case 5: *In one of my interactions, a 94 years old woman* ***Ateola*** *was curious to know how a woman fared in the city. Her interest and curiosity were prompted by the fact that she had never moved out from the village. For the old woman, the world beyond the village is completely unimaginable. She mentioned that her daughter, who lives in the valley (the State capital),* *asked her to come and spent time with her family, even for a short while. To which, she refused saying that her place was nowhere else but in the village. This was, in the past, one glaring example of women.*

When she was a young mother and all her children needed a constant care, she said, her husband would go away to the valley for ***Khayao*** *(labour work). She was a mother of six children, and besides, the duties of childcare, had to take care of her prematurely visually impaired mother-in-law. Whenever her husband left for such trip, she always had to multi-task including that of the normal works of man.*

A comparison of the circumstances of two women, who have mothered at different times, depicts two different pictures. The older women portray the mother who is bounded within the traditional gendered division of labour with duties and responsibilities of household chores and childcare. Her domain is confined within her home and the village. The onus of the younger mother, on the other hand, undeniably represents a different sort of motherhood. She is not pinned within the four walls of the village with unending tasks as the sole caretaker of the household domain as in the past. However, her domestic responsibilities lifted from one shoulder are transferred to the other in the form of financial burden. The former never did set off beyond the village, while the latter moved far and wide, at times, to meet the needs of the family. While placing these premises under the analysis of shouldering responsibilities at home, it gives a lucid manifestation that there are slight changes of gendered division of roles through the years. In other words, it has adapted with the changing needs.

The slight changes observed in the domestic responsibilities is the result coerced by the changing factors in other aspect of their economy, which however should not be mistaken with a complete shift of responsibilities. Because under normal circumstances, women still shoulder the responsibilities of the household chores and the traditional idea that 'a woman's place is in the home' still holds true even in the present context. Though women are seen in different activities outside the domestic arena, the home is still considered as their domain.

This is also true in case of childcare where a mother and the grandmother always take the responsibility of nurturing the young and small children. Though men's roles cannot be routed out in bringing up a child, the overall childcare always rest on women.

There are differences in the age at marriage between women and men. In general, women get married earlier than men. In the past, women would marry at the age of 18-20 while men at the age of 20-25. Today, both men and women marry at an older age. The concept of women to marry at a younger age as compared to men, however, has remained the same. This concept is based on the belief that women should bring forth heirs to the husband as it is considered a disgrace if one could not leave successors for the next generation. This is the logic behind the concept that women should find a groom at the right age when she is at the peak of health in order to avoid the stigma of childlessness. A woman is considered as *larar* (spinster) when she passes the age of 35, which is not the case with men.

In the light of the traditional setup of gender as discussed above, gender learning takes place in the society. The social definition and subsequent self-identification of a child as a boy or as a girl is significant for both the development of gender identity and learning of the way in which one's role performances is tailored to one's gender. Interactions between parents and children, actions of parents and children were taken into account. A discussion on gender identification and learning at different stages of pregnancy and birth, childhood and adolescent period is given hereunder.

PREGNANCY AND BIRTH: Among the Tangkhuls, the concept of childcare starts right from pregnancy. A woman once conceived should restrain from doing certain chores and stay away from visiting certain places with a view to protect the unborn child. Many women, in the village, do not avail themselves of medical facilities to check on the condition of their pregnancy. They would rather depend on the traditional ways of confirming the pregnancy through their beliefs in the biological symptoms like missing of menstrual cycle, aversion to food, mood swing, abdominal bloating, frequent urination, fatigue, nausea, sore breast, etc. Experienced women could easily make out pregnancy signs by looking at the facial changes of a pregnant woman. They narrated experiences with confidence that they could easily make it out by examining the jaw line that becomes lean and skinny.

A young pregnant woman is taught by older ones about diet and food restrictions. There are certain beliefs among the people regarding the foods they eat during pregnancy. Every little detail of what to eat, how to cope with ailments, where and where not to go are imposed on an expectant mother till the baby is delivered, the knowledge of which is passed down from generation to generation. The following are the food restrictions and prohibitions imposed on a pregnant woman, and the explanation for which is based on the traditional beliefs of their culture.

(a) A pregnant woman is forbidden to eat crab, as there is a belief that the baby dribbles all the time.

(b) She is forbidden to kill snakes with a belief that the baby may have the habit of stretching out tongue.

(c) There are prohibitions on certain bitter food items, papaya and prawn, as they consider them harmful for the fetus.

(d) For fear of infliction on the baby by a malevolent spirit, a pregnant woman is not allowed to go out after dark.

(e) She is not allowed to attend funeral services for fear of harm by the spirit of the dead person.

(f) She should keep away from haunted places which they called '*ngalei kharar apam*' as they believe in the presence of malevolent spirits at such places.

These restrictions and taboos are imposed on the mother for the safety of the fetus and the mother. People strictly adhere to this belief. A pregnant woman also ensures herself that her baby is safe from any form of harms. This kind of taboo is not extended to the father of unborn child.

The sex of fetus is predicted through dreams. When a woman in the house is pregnant, all family members share their dreams to predict the sex of the unborn child. Wares, things and objects, associated with each gender, which are seen in dreams, are believed to be the revelation of the child's sex. For instance, if a pregnant woman dreams of any feminine object like weaving implements, baskets, kitchenware, ladies' attires, etc., they believe that the child would be female. In the same way, men's things like axe, spears, men's attire, etc., are considered to be indicative of a male child.

The prediction of sex through dreams is not without patrilineally based favouritism. In a society, where the descent is traced through men, parents always long to have a male child in order to ensure an heir to succeed the father in the family genealogy. This ideology is expressed through verbal lexes and practices. Below are some case studies in this regard.

Case 6: *A year after their marriage,* **Mr** *and* **Mrs Ashang** *were blessed with a baby girl. They were so happy with the arrival of a daughter in the family. A couple of years later, another baby girl came to their life. This time, they were but a bit disappointed— as they have been longing to have a boy, though the family welcomed the second daughter in equal measure.*

As life went by, Mrs. Ashang conceived again. It was during this time, they said— amidst laughter but with a tint of seriousness that they even prayed every day to grant them a son. Every morning, they would discuss and interpret their dreams. And their dreams seem to be in conformity for their preference for a male child. But much against their longings and expectations, a baby girl came again. They were more than disappointed this time— as their wait for an heir to the family had to go on longer.

This time, a serious question lingers in their minds as to what they should do to realise what they have been wishing for. Two years after the third child, the couple came to a decision, buoyed by a desire to have a son, to go for the fourth one.

Case 7: *In the course of my study, I came across scores of gender preferential cases. The focussed group, though within the parameter of young parents, who are raising young children, the case of an elderly couple,* **Mr** *and* **Mrs Ashai** *offered an interesting study. Theirs was a typical case of patrilineal interference in the choice of their children.*

The couple have six daughters. Every pregnancy they waited with a hope to have a son. But their excitement turned to disappointment each time a child was born. The series of events continued till the fifth daughter.

Their hope was shattered when the wife faced difficulty in conceiving a baby. They, however, take consolation looking at the girls growing up, and gradually compromised to carry on their life with the reality of moving on without a son. The sight of lively young girls performing their tasks together was something to be admired of and took away all their worries.

Four years after the birth of the last child, the wife began to show signs of pregnancy. When a morning sickness recurred and she missed her period for more than two months, she could hardly believe the prospect of conceiving at such age. The moment was, however, a silver lining to their long-forgotten dream. But to their dismay, they did not get what they longed for.

Their disappointment was very perceptible in the way they narrated the story. As they grow older, their discontent was further accentuated by the turn of events when the daughters, one after another, began to get married and moved out as customary laws have it with the patrilineal descent. However, they are contented as they are pampered by their daughters with whatever they need.

Case 8: *The case studies were selected from different stories recorded through series of interactions. The experience of Mr.* ***Aho****, a 76 years old, was one typical gender preferential case. In his context, it was not about getting a son but of grandson. The septuagenarian had six children; two sons and two daughters, and all of whom have settled down with their own family. The old couple, as per the customary practice, resides with the eldest son.*

His eldest son was married, but was unfortunately barren. For quite many times, the couple consulted doctors and tried every possible means to have a child. They even consulted a ***Khanong*** *(a traditional medical practitioner). But it also did not yield any result. Though on seeing their hapless effort, the old man could not do anything but sigh with despair.*

The old man looked upon his second son for a grandson, who would take over the name of the family and stand in the genealogy of the family tree. He would advise him, time and again, to take every possible care in choosing a life partner. As the family's descent was at stake, he would even ask his son to get married early. When his son came home one day to take the consent of the parents, the news was welcomed with great joy. The first child came along, and it fulfilled the cherished dream of the whole family. The old man was finally blessed with a grandson son.

Cases as such are very prevalent among the Tangkhuls. This is one aspect of their practices which is very obvious of their gender preferences. So, the imprint of patrilineal descent draws its own picture in the minds of the people that come out in the portrait of their practices. However, the picture of male preference does not imply that girls are unwanted. They have a strong feeling that there is no homeliness without daughters. Though preference of a male child is a necessity in this patrilineal society, they yearn for equal gender composition with both male and female. Following are case studies depicting their longing for a female child.

***Case 9:** I was observing how **Mrs. Akui** had been passing compliments to some mothers— of how lucky they are to have daughters. Her remarks to young girls, who came by to fetch water from the community water reservoir, were very apparent of her desire to have a daughter. She would tell them how fortunate their mothers were to have girls like them. I observed and perused her remarks, and drew my conclusion that she did not have a daughter. I visited her to verify my hypothesis drawn from the premises of her comments.*

My assumption was verified, and I put up her case under my studies. Stringing every bits and pieces of her story, a lucid picture of why a family is not complete without a daughter could be framed in this patrilineal society.

***Asa** lived in a nuclear family. As her husband was the third son, her in-laws lived in separate houses. Until the arrival of the second child, her chores at home were light and manageable. She had to perform her duties and responsibilities as a mother of two young children, and as the sole caretaker of all the chores at home. Her husband, a working person, could hardly assist her.*

In her times, there was no practice of keeping a help at home. Mothers were considered as homemakers to handle all sorts of duties. The family used to reside in the district headquarters those days, and could least expect help from their relatives. The arrival of the third son made her life more hectic. In addition to attending and nursing an infant, she had to take care of the older boys, who also needed constant care and monitoring.

At this point of time, the couple felt the need to have a daughter who could lend a helping hand to the mother. As the couple watched the boys play without care, they felt that girls of their age would have been more helpful in the house, a societal concept that 'boys will be boys'—who should be given their space to be naughty; while girls be trained to be more patient and maintain restraint with their behaviour.

The fourth son came, followed by another, and so on till the sixth one. But soon after the birth of her sixth son, her husband was taken ill and bedridden. The father passed away when the youngest child was only six-month-old. As a single parent she brought up her sons, while multitasking her duties and chores at home and outside. Her experience, as a young mother, always stayed fresh in her mind and her unfulfilled desire still linger in her mind. The sight of young girls assisting their mothers and performing the household chores reminds her of the longing that never was fulfilled.

Case 10: *In the contemporary Tangkhul society, the concept of birth control is not a new concept. It was the lack of medical facility that kept the people from availing the services.*

The case of ***Mr. Mayo*** *represents an inimitable instance worth considering when it comes to girl child preference. The family falls in the category of middle income group of economic division. The couple are well aware of birth control and easy access to medical services. They have six sons and a daughter, who is the youngest among the siblings. In the present time, to raise such a number of children posed certain challenges on economic fronts.*

For the couple, it was indeed unplanned to have such a big family. They have wanted and waited for a daughter after the birth of the second son. Their expression made me curious as I had come across many cases of patrilineal influence in the mindset of the people that placed a male child on priority list. They justified that a family is never complete without equal gender composition of children. Though they considered sons are the necessity for inheritance according to their customary laws, a home without a daughter lacks the warmth and homeliness. It was owing to this reason that the family ended with seven children.

Case 11: *There is hardly any adherent now, amongst the younger generation, for a big family. So, people go for small family with the changing times. There are however certain cases, where the number of children cannot be maintained as planned, and the reason for which is gender preference— as one would sum it up. This was the case with one of my informants,* ***Ashim****. She has three kids; two sons and a daughter, which according to the standard of parents in the present time, would call it the right gender composition. She is a happy young mother today, who at one point of time has had a tormenting experience of losing her first daughter.*

Three years after the birth of her sons, she was blessed with a daughter. To have a girl child after two sons was a joyous moment for the couple. They were so overjoyed, and pampered her with lots of love and care. However, their happiness was short-lived when her daughter began to show symptoms of sickness, every now and then. The couple's fear grew stronger with increasing signs of multiple ailments. I could feel her grief as she was narrating her agonizing experience.

The mother dedicated all her time to the ailing child, and sometimes could not help but shed silent tears. The couple tried every possible means to save their daughter's life. But, all their efforts were in vain. Their only daughter passed away at a very tender age.

Losing a daughter was the saddest moment for the couple. They felt a stark emptiness at home, however hard they tried to console themselves. Whenever she saw a mother with her girl child, she felt a deep void in her life. She was but hopeful of conceiving again. She waited and waited but it did not happened even after many years. At a time when all hopes seemed to have vanished into thin air, she conceived again after a gap of eight years. Much to the happiness of the family, this time again, she gave birth to a daughter.

The case studies presented above give two pictures of gender preferences; a depiction of gender structure dichotomized by the patriliny where a male child is preferred over a female child and another image portraying the need for a female child to complete the circle of a warm and lively family. Male preference arises out of the bare necessity to continue their descent which forms the core of their culture. The reason is attributed to the fact that daughters are not entitled to uphold the family's tradition. This is certainly the reason why a male child is preferred over a female child.

A female child preference is suggestive that a girl is not an unwanted child in a family. Daughters represent as the symbol of homeliness. The case studies have made it clear that there is always a void without a girl child, which can never be filled by sons. However, it is evident that people do not place equal values to a male child and a female child, which is accountable to the patrilineal structure of the society.

Within the given milieu of the concepts and practices of gender during pregnancy, an examination on the practices of birth and childcare would throw more light on gender socialisation of the Tangkhul society.

Birth

As soon as a child is born, a hot water therapy is administered to the baby by the midwife or by the grandmother. Relatives, friends and neighbours come with gifts in the form of chicken and clothes for the baby and the mother. According to their belief, the mother recovers from the labour soreness and fatigue on the sixth day in case of birthing a boy and on a fifth day in case of girl. During this period, the mother is regularly administered hot water therapy known as "*phasa khangalui*". A thick cloth, soaked in hot water, is wrapped over her body. It is then followed by steaming process where a piece of cloth soaked in hot water is pressed all over her body. This is a therapeutic treatment to ensure infection-free and speedy recovery from delivery.

After a week, a ritual is performed known as "*naoyan,*" which literally means 'seeing the baby' for the first time. It is a way of declaring the arrival of the baby. For this particular ritual, a fat rooster is gifted by the maternal uncle or grandfather of the baby (in case of a boy). The chicken is then cooked and distributed to all the relatives and neighbours to mark the "*naoyan*". The chicken distributed on the occasion of *naoyan* is known as "*naoyansa*", which means 'baby seeing meat'. In this regard, killing of rooster symbolises that the baby grows up to be a dutiful man to awaken all the people as a rooster does in the morning.

The ritual is symbolical of exposing the baby to outsiders. It is customary for parents and family members to keep the newly born infant away from visitors and outsiders. This belief is associated with the fear of malevolent spirit which could disturb the wellbeing of the small infant. They have strong belief in the existence of *mirai kakaza*; a belief that some people possess powers of inflicting harm to another person. Till today, they adhere to this belief and have a dreading attitude to the power associated with it. As such, the infant is kept away from outsiders as they believe that infants are vulnerable to such infliction. The mother, prior to the ritual, is advised to take bed rest.

The ritual, from the perspective of gender, offers a symbolical vista of their gendered social matrix. The interference of primogeniture shows eminence with spotlights given to the *naoyan* of the first-born son. Observance of the ritual is mandatory on the arrival of the first son. However, in case of a girl child, the ritual may even be given amiss. If at all this ritual is taken up for a daughter, a strict rule of gift in the form of rooster from the maternal uncle is not necessarily maintained. Thus, the ritual is characteristic of their patriliny.

0 – 5 Years

During infancy, the baby spends much of the time with the mother and the paternal grandmother. In the first few weeks, the infant is given a hot water therapy known as '*nao khangalui*' (this is similar to the therapy administered to the mother mentioned earlier). It is believed to be a therapeutic treatment for strong immunity, growth and strength.

There is also a common belief that evil spirit can harm the baby if proper name is not given to the child at an early stage. This occasion is known as *'naoming kaphok'* – name giving ceremony. In the past, the priest took charge of this ceremony where a feast was given to the relatives, friends and neighbours. However, the ritual which was in practice earlier is now replaced by a ceremony in the Church where the pastor or priest prays for the child. In some cases, a feast is given by the parents of the child by inviting the pastor to perform the ceremony at home. The name may be given by the parents or they may ask the elderly person of the family, friends and relatives to give a meaningful name of their choice. However, the name of baby should have certain significance and relevance to the family or the society. Following are some instances of names and meanings associated with them.

Phangreiwon – The literal meaning of the name can be translated with each syllable; '*Phang*' as branch, '*rei*' as large and '*won*' as flower. The significance of the name is chosen from the marital ties of the parents. The maternal grandfather is the clan's chief. As such, the name is indicative of the mother's background to show that the girl is the descendant of the clan's chief denoted by the term, 'main branch' (*Phang-rei*) with the feminine suffix, '*won*'.

Sinmi - The boy was born at the time when his father got his job while the grandfather retired on superannuation. The name thus has an economic significance. The word, *'Sin'* is a syllable summarised from the word '*lansin*' meaning economy (financial aspect), while '*mi*' meaning give or bestow. The name, as such, is a connotation of handing over the job of the grandfather to the child's father.

Phungshimpam – The name is a nuance of the family royal status as they are descendants of the village chief. The literal meaning in syllable can be read as *'Phung'* meaning rule, '*shim*' meaning sweet to denote 'sweet relationship' and '*pam*' meaning reside. In this context, the name signifies a pledge that all the family members live together, stick together and rule the village under one umbrella.

The names of the Tangkhul have easy gender identification suffixes. Generally, the suffix '*la*', '*phy*' or '*won*' is added at the end of a girl's name to designate their gender. Boys' name, on the other hand, does not have these suffixes.

The occasion of *naoming kaphok* (name giving ceremony) is usually simple today as mentioned earlier with a prayer in the church or with a special meal of the family. However, *naoming kaphok* of the eldest son is still an occasion of feast and celebration. This, however, is not applicable in case of a girl child even if she happens to be the eldest. The importance bestowed to the eldest son can be attributed to its birth right as upholder of the family's tradition, which is noteworthy of their patrilineal system and specifically of their custom of primogeniture.

Before a child can accurately identify himself or herself as *ngalanao* (girl) or *mayarnao* (boy), the child receive a range of clues. For instance, adult men and women handle the infant boy/girl differently, systematic differences in dress and hairstyle and formulate visual clues for an infant in the learning process. An adult who handles a small infant boy would often say "*mayarnaona machap paimanei*", which indicates 'boys do not cry', while on the other hand, to console a baby girl takes one to say "*ishi ngalanaoli khipana chap ngasakda*", which means 'who makes our girl cry?' The statement bears a range of gendered connotation. The undertone signifies that boys are nurtured to be emotionally strong while expressing the tradition that women are being protected. The society thus sanctions different values to each gender as construed through such verbal clues.

Gendered label is also apparent in hair dressing among the Tangkhuls. Traditionally, boys shave their hair on the sides, leaving a patch of hair from the front till the back of the head — the hairdo is known as *Hao kuiret*. Girls used to keep fringe cut at the front known as *samkok*. They keep the hair a little longer at the sides to cover the ear and long lock on the rear. However, when they attain a marriageable age, they let the front hair grows. As such a distinguishing mark was maintained among the girls to indicate their status based on their age. Though the hairstyles have evolved over the years, a distinguishing mark still continue to segregate each gender where women keep long hair and men go for short haircut. This way the child is given clues to identity through differences in their hairstyle.

Differences in dressing are another way of streamlining gender variation to the small child. A man would never be seen with women's clothes like skirt, *kashan* (wrap-around lower garment), ladies tops, etc. The traditional attires too are strictly gendered though these are not for everyday use. Besides observation of children on gender dress codes, parents and elders contour gender dress code on them through the way they dress them up. This goes on till the children can pick their own choice of clothes and do their own hairstyle.

Internalisation of gender values by a child, during this stage, is marked by role imitation in the way they talk and play. The message is clear as I watch them play imitating the role of their specific gender. Small girls are seen playing with dolls in their own imaginary kitchen. Small boys of this age group take the role of adult men as they engaged themselves with their play session. They are seen taking the role of shopkeepers, carpenters, drivers, etc. Sometimes they could be seen demarcating their status as father, mother, brother and sister, according to their respective gender. The roles imitation of children in itself represents the roles of their adults.

Values of what constitute masculinity or femininity in their emotions are also given clues through the language of parents and elders. Statement like "*Mayarnaona machap paimanei*", which means 'boys do not cry' and "*Mayarnao chi mayarnao laka*", which suggests "boys will always be boys" indicates the way elders shape the sentiments of young boys. A boy who comes running home with minor injury would be told to bear the pain saying 'boys will be boys'. The same act committed by a girl, however, has a different connotation— the small girl would be consoled by saying 'who made my child cry' or 'who hurt my baby', or she would be told to be more careful next time. This way elders silhouette the emotions of the young minds to the dichotomized gender values of the society.

Toys, which a young child possesses, tend to emphasise between male or female attribute. For instance, a boy plays with *kari* (toy vehicles made of wood or purchased from market), *sayur* (toy animals made of clay or wood) and girls are seen with *nga-nganao* (dolls) and *thangthang* (toy kitchenwares), which they make collections out of used bottles and other items). Practically, all children in fact possess and play with gendered toys given to them by parents, relatives and well-wishers. The response to such gender stereotyping also comes from parents and elders, where toys are categorically purchased for a boy child and a girl child. For instance, if a boy played with kitchen toys or dolls, elders chided him saying, "*na ngalanaola*?" which means 'are you a girl?' or if a girl took a ride on a *thingkari* (a cycle assembled from wooden structures), elders would say "*ngalanaowui ot maningmana*," which means 'it is not a girl's plaything.' Even in their treatment towards children, they show gender stereotyping as girls are not allowed to play with boy's toys and vice versa.

Children at this stage spend much of their time at home, and that too, mostly with their grandparents whenever their parents are away to the fields. The circle of friends is formed among the neighbourhood children. Most children start attending school at the age of five and thus spend longer period of the day in school. However, socialisation, at this stage, takes place mostly within the family.

As the child learns to identify his or her gender, they also pick up gender specific terms like *'shanao'* (women), *'mayarnao'* (men) and learn to identify others' gender too. Some simple kinship terminologies like *ava* - mother, *ani* - aunt, *amei* - elder brother, *achon* - elder sister, etc. are taught to them. The basic knowledge of who they are is thus inculcated into the young minds during this period.

6 – 12 Years

Given the label to a person as a boy or a girl based on their biological anatomy, the society imposes expectations on the individual to behave and act according to their gender and not to deviate from it. It is in the practices of everyday life that these expectations are fulfilled and reproduced. For instance, a boy of six years is expected to learn the role of running errands among other things. A girl of the same age is expected to learn household chores, attend to younger children and so on.

Even if there are no hard and fast rules of streamlining the gender division of labour, there is always a line of demarcation. **Mrs *Zingyinla***, one of my informants, would not rely on her son to baby-sit the younger siblings. She also complained that if the sons do the dishes, they frequently break the kitchen wares. In the same way, girls are not allowed to do carpentry work or chop firewood. So, the children do not have equal access to all kinds of works and this is simply based on gendered division of labour. Thus, children within this age category learn to play their role appropriate to their own gender and gender demarcation becomes apparent.

The nature of gendered division of labour, however, deviates from the usual norm in some exceptional cases of families with one gender composition of children. For instance, there are families with only boys or some other families with only girl children. In such context, division of labour give different picture as can be referred from the following case studies.

Case ***12*****:** ***Angamla*** *was widowed at a very young age. When her husband passed away, she was still nursing her third daughter. Now left with no man in the house, she would often ask for helping hands from her own three brothers to which they would willingly comply. In spite of their unrelenting care and concern, she decided to manage on her own as far as possible as she could not be a burden to them all the time.*

"I try to pick up the skills to attend to any wear and tear at home, which otherwise would have been mostly handled by my husband," she related during our interactions.

Her three daughters, who were between seven to thirteen years of age, also assisted the mother in whatever way they could at home and in the fields. The girls would, during their holidays, help the mother in the field with spade works and fencing. At home, they would also assist the mother in fixing and repairing of chicken coops, kitchen drainage and shelves. The girls would also run errands for the mother which otherwise would have been performed by boys.

The young widow has full of appreciation for her daughters. She praised them as they are a blessing in more ways than one. She stated that her daughters from very young age could pick up so many tasks, which otherwise are basically considered a man's trade.

The mother and her daughters perform duties and tasks, which otherwise are categorised as responsibilities of men in other families simply because they do not have men in the family. In another case study, I came across a family with only sons whose response to gender division of labour creates a different picture as they learn their duties.

Case ***13*****:** *It is a rare scene to witness a man doing dishes in the kitchen among the Tangkhul families, as this household chore is considered a women's task in their division of labour. I came across this isolated case during a visit to a house for data collection, which prompted me to undertake the instance as a case study.*

***Mr** and **Mrs Luingam** have four sons. The parents would hardly allow them to spend their leisure time like any the other boys of their age, who would be seen with friends playing in the neighbourhood. As the mother could not manage the chores all by herself, the tasks were assigned to each of the boys. While her 12-year old **Ngamshang** assisted in floor-mopping and the dishes, his elder brother who is fond of cooking, would join the mother in the kitchen. The younger siblings would do the housekeeping including sweeping, room-cleaning and laundry. With no daughter in the family, the boys were compelled to pick up girl's tasks— which otherwise would have been different under normal circumstances.*

The above cases depict a different picture outside the society's norms of gendered division of labour. In a family without daughters, boys perform the duties of girls like mopping the floor, doing the dishes, washing their clothes and sweeping the floors. The same goes the other way round in families without sons. However, these are some exceptional cases which are not applicable to the conventional gendered division of labour.

Generally, it is observed that parents assign duties and responsibilities to girls that require more time and patience. Their duties like cleaning, washing and cooking keep them more occupied as compared to boys.

Values of masculinity and femininity are manifested in different ways through socialisation process. There is a popular saying, *"mayarnaona khama khangakhai khangachana,"* which means it is natural for boys to bear wounds. This is a typical portrayal of masculine value of daring character which engaged men in risky ventures. It is manifested in the behaviour of children at play. Boys tend to play rough games exposing them to higher risk, which is why boys are expected to bear more wounds and bruises on their body. Girls, on the other hand, tend to be more careful with their physical movements and refrain themselves from dangerous activities. As it is evident from the saying mentioned above, elders use this axiom to instill courageous personality to boys. Girls, on the other hand, are guided to keep away from perilous actions. For instance, girls are not encouraged to ride the wood-assembled cycle meant for boys or climb trees.

In the process of imparting gender specific roles, the mother and other female members of the family take the growing girl child under their supervision and monitor young girls in learning the feminine trade. Elder men do the same for boys in imparting the masculine role. Therefore, the role imitation in the play session during their early years gradually turns into role learning as they reach this stage. Simultaneously, the children learn responsibilities too. Children of this age group begin to take different tasks appropriate to their gender.

Gender segregation also takes place in this age group. As they become conscious of their own gender, they feel shy and uncomfortable to mix with the opposite gender which results in formation of groups within one's own sex. Thus, an individual is socialised into the circle of their own gender and they gradually learn to adjust with their friends.

Apart from socialisation within the family, the children now go beyond their courtyard and spend their leisure hours with their friends. The games, at this stage, are gender specific which is played within the circle of their own gender. Some traditional games are discussed as follows:

Girls:

Saotheila (Throwing Knuckle Bones): It is a game where as many as twenty girls can participate in two groups. This game is played by using *Saothei* — a flat, round seed extracted from a creeper's plant called *Saorong* in local parlance. The game consists of passing through various levels. Each group compete to win the game by completing the final stage of the game using diverse techniques.

Kotla (Game of Five Stones): A game which is more or less similar to the game commonly known as five stones. Here, the girls gather small pebbles and play the game in groups or in duo. It is a game where girls sit together and play using their hands to flip and pick up the stones in varying patterns.

Boys:

Mahar Kapai: It is a traditional game of high-jump. The name originates from the word '*mahar*' – a kind of small tall plant, which is used in the game as poles and marking lines, and the word '*kapai*', which means jumping or flying. In this game, the boys would compete among themselves to take the highest jump. Two poles would be erected opposite to the other with a distance of about two metres. The poles have branches at equal interval for placing a horizontal bar as a marking line of height for the jumper. The height would be raised higher after each round and participants who failed to jump over the line would be eliminated. The participant who could take the highest jump is the winner of the game.

Sao Katak: This game involves a top made of wood, which has a spherical body that tapers towards the lower part to form a sharp edge and an upper end with a small round tip for a thin string to be strapped over. The rope is pulled abruptly to make it spin. Group of boys spin their own *sao* together and exhibit their art. The top is spun allowing it to hit others' *sao*. The last standing *sao* is the winner of the game.

The games each gender play exhibit different characteristics. Girls play games which are physically less challenging and of more indoor type. Game like *saotheila* is an outdoor game but this game is played within a limited yard. Whereas, *kotla* is an indoor game where they have to sit and play inside the house or under a shady tree. On the other hand, the nature of boy's games is more stressful. It requires energy and is mainly of an outdoor type. For instance, *mahar kapai* is a physically challenging game in which they have to jump and balance their body simultaneously. When the player is off balance, it may even sometimes result to injury. The girl's games show that they play safe. On the contrary, boys who are scared to take challenges are ridiculed as *malung makazang* (coward) and *ngalakaphem* (sissy). These games give certain pictures of the gender relations among the people – the values attached to boys as rough and daring, and girls as patient and tender.

Gender socialisation, at this stage, incorporates learning of one's place in the kinship network. Among the Tangkhuls, the whole social system revolves around the kinship organisation. A person is identified by the village to which she or he belongs. One is again recognised with his or her clan and is further subsumed under the family. As such all through the lifecycle, a person's actions are bound by obligations and reciprocal relationship of the kinship organisation.

As the children reach this stage, they are taught by the family elders to understand as to where they belong in the kinship network. They are explained as to why they should address people by different terminologies. The genealogy of the *shimkhur* (family), the *meiphung* (lineage) and the *shangnao* (clan) are taught to them by the elders. For instance, a child is explained as to who he or she should call *'avakatui'* (mother's younger sister) and to differentiate the relationship with the paternal aunts whom they refer to as '*ani*'. The children, thus, gradually understand why and how they are related to others.

The children are taught, within the capacity of their understanding, the patrilineal and patriarchal values of the society – the descent traced through men and the family under the headship of men. They begin to understand the system of culture where men continue to remain in the family while women move out to become other family after marriage. The status of each individual in the family and in the wider social network is taught to them by elders. For instance, a girl before her marriage enjoys the status as a *naongalava* (daughter) in her natal home which is switched to the status of *apareiva* or *ava* (wife or mother) after marriage. The change of status is taught side by side with the change of identity from one clan to another. A man, on the other hand, changes his identity from a son to *agahara* (husband) and *ava* (father) with marriage and sustains the tradition of the family in their kinship network. This way, children learn their place in the social grid of their culture.

A unique feature of cultural transmission among the Tangkhul is the age-old oral tradition, which is indeed a fundamental agent of cultural continuity. This tradition, though not as dynamic as in the past, still finds an important place in gender socialisation and in the process of value transmission. Children of this age group have not attained the stage to understand the customs and practices analytically. Gender specific qualities of what the society considers good or bad is narrated to them in the form of *awo-ayi khararchan* (folktales). Following are some folktales that were recorded from such narrators who take the role of social chronicles in order to examine symbolic representation of gender values that are built and woven into the folktales.

Khabe

Once there lived in a village, a widow and her only son, Khabe. The mother loved him so much as she was loved by him. The inseparable bond became the talk of the village. For the mother, it was a painful challenge to stay away from her only child. Whenever she had to go to the fields, the young boy would either be kept under the care of her trusted neighbours or relatives. On many occasions, the mother would return home halfway from the fields to be with her son.

Time passed by. Khabe had also come of age. Then a day came, his mother asked him to get married. Thus, Khabe brought home a girl. And, the three lived together.

For some time, they lived a normal and happy life. But, the happiness of his mother was but short-lived. She began to suffer undue treatment in the hands of her daughter-in-law. It happened whenever the husband was not at home. Whenever Khabe was away from the village, his mother would be sent to the jhum all alone. For days and nights together, she would toil in the field. Then the daughter-in-law would send unusual inedible foodstuffs to her mother-in-law who was toiling in the fields. In an utter show of mistreatment, the daughter-in-law would pack Zatkang (burnt rice), Theithukthei (wild apples as meat) and Samra (leftover water from rinsing rice— as rice beer) for her.

Khabe's mother could not muster the courage to speak about the matter to him. So much was her love for the son that she did not dare bother him with her complaint. So, she would often quench her thirst and hunger by drinking water from the nearby stream, and ate whatever was found in nearby surroundings. This went on for quite some time.

Nevertheless, the mother never loses heart. She would tend the jhum diligently. But Khabe's wife was never satisfied, and would often find ways to chide her. Many a time, she would also throw her disapproval in the way Khabe's mother tended the fields.

So, at times, when the mother felt lonesome and sad, she would hum a song—

Khape-da naolikhi liu mavathe, lanwo,

Khi vanaoka yamthen kano, yamshot dei,

O Khabe!

English version:

(When Khabe was young,

I'd often returned home, halfway from the field.

Never had I lured in the birds to the field,

but always shooed away.

O Khabe!)

Early one morning, Khabe returned home from khayao (labour trip). He told his wife that he would be going to the fields, and then asked her to pack food for his mother. Within no time, he was headed to the fields. As Khabe reached the viewpoint of the field, he crooned (kakaho) loudly giving signal to his mother of his arrival. The mother heard the voice, and thought that it resembled that of her son. She however ignored it as she did not expect him at the odd hour of the day, until he appeared by the hut. He called out to his mother to come and eat the food brought from home. But, the mother gently refuses to eat. She then asked her son to look what is beneath the Tarong (a platform built alongside the hut).

Khabe found three holes dug into the ground. To his utter surprise, there were Zatkang, Samra and Theithukthei put separately in each hole. On seeing this, his anger knew no bound. Immediately, he escorted her home.

When they reached the courtyard of their house, Khabe told her to enter the house alone. As soon as she walked into the kitchen, the daughter-in-law began to chide and insult her. Then, Khabe coughed and entered the kitchen pretending not to know anything of the insults meted out to his mother. His wife then put up her pretence, and served him rice beer with a bowl of meat.

Khabe asked his wife to soak the kashai (a rope used for carrying basket) in water. The wife did exactly as she was told. After he was done with his drinks, he asked his wife to bring him the kashai. Then as his wife brought the rope, he whipped her.

The folktale carries an underlying theme of gender ideals as we analyse the story. The wife is depicted as a woman who flouts the norms of an ideal *arihava* (daughter-in-law). The husband, on the other hand, is the figure of a patriarch whose authority is supreme in the family. This kind of tales plays its role to instil gendered ideals in which we could apparently perceive how the core values are transmitted to the young minds.

The interplay of internalising the value patriarchy and patriliny is revealed eloquently in another such commonly told folktale. The story goes like this:

Liuyakla and Liukanpha

Once there lived a man by the name Liukanpha. He married Liuyakla, after courting her for some years. A year after their marriage, they were blessed with a son. They were so happy, and took care of the child with all the love and affection as much as they cared for each other.

The couple lived a happy life and the villagers talked profoundly about the family.

One day, they had a serious argument. Liuyakla walked out of the house, leaving behind her husband and child. She refused to return home even after so much of repeated persuasion. So, Liukanpha had no choice, but to take care of the child all by himself.

Liuyakla loved her young child so much so that she would sometime come by and watch him play from distance. Occasionally, she would also come to take a peek from the neighbourhood, to see how the father and son were doing at home. Every time, the mother saw her son, it would break her heart with a longing to hold him in her arms.

Liukanpha learnt about what Liuyakla had been up to. So, whenever he sensed her presence in the vicinity of the house, the father would pamper the child in all the way he could to show that he could fare it all by himself. Sometime, the father and the son would be in playful mood. He would keep a meat on one end of the bed, and fish on the other. The child would then be asked to run along from one end to the other, and endeared himself with the delicacies.

The sight of her husband and son made the mother so happy. At the same time, she would also feel remorseful and envious to see them together in such playful mood and happiness without her.

One day, Liukanpha, on sensing the presence of Liuyakla around the house, tried to provoke her with a song. He thus sang—

"Oh inao samthiri, Liuyakla! Liuyakla! Maleishishilo!

(Oh my son has just began to walk; Liuyakla (2x) does not love him).

On hearing the song, she could no longer hold her emotions. From the place where she was hiding, she replied—

"Oh khisa maleikashino, Liuyakla, Liuyakla maung khaloine!

(Oh why shouldn't I love my son! But Liuyakla(2x) is not coming back).

Liukanpha then picked up his spear, and threw at the direction from where the song came. From that day on, she never came to see them again.

The story depicts the rights of the father over the children. In Tangkhul society, a mother can never claim her rights over her children whatever the circumstance may be. The child is always affiliated to the father's clan. The story depicts the love of a mother to her child. It portrays a helpless woman, who despite her love for the child has to give up all hopes of claiming the child.

Exploring on different themes of folktales through the spectrum of gender, another such folktales is narrated as follows.

A Girl and a Bear

There was once a beautiful lady who lived in a village. Her beauty was admired by all in the village and words of her gorgeous elegance spread beyond the boundary of the village.

When the daughter had come of age for marriage, the father put up a challenge to all the prospective grooms who came asking for her hand in marriage. The contest was to slaughter a pig with a single blow. He declared that his daughter would be given to a man who could perform the feat.

Words spread fast and many young men from near and far came to try their luck to win the hand of the girl in marriage. One after another, they took up the challenge which indeed became an impossible task as no one could succeed in their attempt. Until one day, a young man turned up and asked the father to give him a chance with the challenge. As any other man who put up a good display with their performance, he entered the pig sty. Much to the astonishment of the onlookers, he accomplished the task with ease.

The father, as promised, gave away her daughter in marriage without any hesitation as he was so pleased with the performance of the young man. With much pomp and gaiety in the village, a feast was given as they bade farewell to the beautiful lass.

The bride, according to the customary practices, would be escorted to the groom's village by friends and family in cases of inter-village marriage. As such, they made preparation the next morning. The man however stopped the father-in-law that it would be a long journey. He further explained to them that it would be inconvenient for the escort party to undergo such a long tiring trip and insisted on taking the girl all by himself. Finally, he convinced the family that he would take good care of their beloved daughter and that she would be loved and cared for.

The couple started the long journey which never seemed to end. The girl kept on asking how further they have to travel as she was exhausted to which he always replied that they are about to reach.

It was dusk as they stood staring at the fading glow of the horizon. The girl asked the man if they have to walk further. This time he replied affectionately that they have reached home, and that she should trust him and do what he asked of her. He told the girl to close her eyes and open it only when she is asked to do so. He then transformed into a bear and carried her on his back. Without letting her know, he climbed up the old giant tree which he called home. On reaching the top, he turned back into his human form, and told her to open her eyes. Taken over by fatigue, the girl dozed off.

The next morning when the girl woke up, she found herself on top of a tree house in the middle of a dense forest. The unfamiliar surrounding took her by surprise and she was shocked beyond words. She began to panic but her conscience told her to keep her composure. Gathering all her equanimity, she tried to talk to him in order to find out his background. As one would expect, he ignored her queries and climbed down a rope on the pretext of collecting food. He then asked his wife to untie the end of the rope, and drop it on the ground for him. This was done to ensure that the wife never leave their tree house.

By and by, the wife began to notice unusual habits of the man leaving her suspicious of his every move. When the husband says he would be back before sunset, he usually returns by nightfall. And the day he tells her that he would be late, she could expect him before dusk.

With time, she drew up her plans. She had to find out why she was kept captive and about the man she married to. She asked her husband to bring a particular bark of shrubs saying that she needs them to make rugs in order to kill her boredom. To her surprise, the man would bring bundles every day. Overtly, she would pretend to weave rugs while discreetly she would knit a seipheng khara (a rope made of yarned bark) strong and long enough for her to get down from the tree house.

One fine day, when the husband said that he would be home early, she took the opportunity to execute her plan. After the husband descended to the ground, she followed him and stalked behind to find out where he used to go and what he used to do. He stopped at a field, and she hid herself on the trunk of a big tree. To her utter dismay, he transformed himself into a bear and began digging out the taro (Yam) with his claws. Snuffing her screams with her shawl, she sneaked away as fast as she could. In between sobs, she ran as far as her shaky legs could take her.

While putting up a normal act as any other day, the woman began to haste up her escape plan as each day with her so called husband was filled with fear and disgust, and it began to feel like forever. Every day, she would nag her husband to bring fig on the pretext that she has strong appetite for it. She would pilfer some in the corner basket and hid it until it was too heavy for her to carry.

One fateful day, when her husband left home saying he would be home before sunset, she sets off with her basketful of figs. She knew the husband would come after her. The figs she carried along was intended to slow him down, as she knew too well that the husband would not mind stopping for few bites of fig with salt and powdered chili pepper. She thus placed a handful of figs with a pinch of salt and pepper at regular intervals along the route. As she scurried along, her load lightened as the figs were placed along the way.

When her husband returned, a rope hanging from the tree house immediately raised alarm. He did not expect that the wife would be able to escape from him. With the hope to catch up with his wife, he followed her tracks hastily. As anticipated, his swift pace was punctuated by the sight of figs with salt and chili pepper. He thus spent few moments here and there, relishing the fruit placed along the way.

As expected the next morning, the man turned up at his father-in-law's house. The father-in-law, on the other hand, had come up with a plan after much deliberation throughout the night. He gave him a warm reception announcing other members of the family that his son-in-law had come to pay him a visit. Putting up with all his jovial act, he declared that he would welcome the visit by slaughtering a pig. So, he called upon the son-in-law and asked him to drag out the stout and biggest pig.

As exhibited in his feat to get the consent of marriage, the man skillfully caught hold of the pig by its hind legs and dragged it out. Then, the girl's father swung his lethal haphang (a wooden handle of an axe) but missed the intended target. In the spurt of the moment, the man let off the pig from his hold. Then, his father-in-law quickly apologized for his clumsy actions, and convinced him that he would not miss the target again. This time the girl's father hit him right on his forehead and took him down with a single blow. The man growled and writhed in pain and gradually transformed into a bear, and collapsed on the ground.

The girl's father butchered the bear into pieces and let it dry on Phungshar (a suspended bamboo rack right above the hearth).

One evening as the girl was cooking, a drop of warm oil from the bear's meat trickled down from the Phungshar and smeared her arms.

Few days later, the girl woke up in the morning to find herself inflicted with skin inflammation all over her body. With the sores getting worse each day, her parents decided to keep her away from the house. They left her alone in a room attached to a granary— some distance away from the house. The little brother who loved her dearly could not bear to watch her. So, he would pack her favourite dishes and give her company from distance, every morning and evening.

One day, as the boy was mowing the grasses beneath the floor of his sister's hut, he killed a snake. He then told her sister about it and headed home. After a while, the girl got curious and peeped through the bamboo floor to take a look at the dead snake. She saw a male snake slithering around the dead one. The sight was so unusual that it totally caught her whole attention. She watched with great attention to find out what would happen next.

After a little while, the male snake slithered away. It came back with a leaf with which the male snake smeared it over the still body of the female snake by twitching and twisting his body around the dead snake. To her utter surprise, the dead snake came to life.

The next day when her brother turned up with the food package, she immediately asked him to pluck the particular leaves. The girl crushed the leaves in between her palms and applied them all over her infected skin. Few days later, she could see signs of recovery as her skin cleared up.

One bright sunny day, she went to a nearby spring to fetch water. It was at that moment she met a young and handsome man, who happened to be a son of a neighbouring village chief. He fell so much in love with the girl and won her hearts. They eventually got married.

She would remember her brother fondly all the while, as she recalled how he cared for her when no one wanted to come near her. So, she invited him to come visit her. He came and stayed with the sister and they had a good time. Before leaving, he was asked to pick a buffalo of his choice from the herd as a token of love and gratitude.

However, he had been advised by his sister, who had learnt the secret of her husband's cattle, to pick the leanest from the herd. He picked as he was told. The prince was taken aback, and was prompted to ask his brother-in-law if he had made the right choice. To this, the boy replied affirmatively. The boy then took off with the buffalo and returned home.

The lean skinny buffalo began to give healthy calves and some years later, he had a large herd of buffaloes. He then realised why his sister had advised him to go for the leanest among the herd. He thus became the richest man in his village, which was indeed a reward for his love and loyalty towards his sister.

The story depicts how a father tried to find a groom for his daughter without a background check on the man, which is a vital prerequisite criterion in choosing a son-in-law or a husband. Through the folktale, the consequences of disregarding tradition are infused to the young minds. The story also portrays the duties and responsibilities of a brother towards his sister and the reciprocity of love and affection between a brother and sister. Through the story, the reciprocal kin ties of gender are demonstrated.

A very significant socialisation process I witnessed, which indeed appears to be negligible at the outset of the investigation, is gender values elders inculcate to children implicitly through their discussion and mundane talk. The discussion always juxtaposes notions of gender values through characters of people. Every family would be seen sitting around the fireplace after an evening meal which may be referred to as family time, as this is the only time they get to sit together in the context of a typical village life. Some value-oriented stories and anecdotes on gender I learnt during such conversations are related here under.

Case 14**:** *The Tangkhuls have a tradition of expressing their sentiments in an overt form over the demise of near and dear ones. They keep good memories of a dead person very close to their hearts, and it is so apparent in the way they talk for days, months and years. A conversation with a family, one evening by a fireside, brings out the story of* ***Atipnao****, a 35-year-*

old widow. It was a week after the demise of her mother-in-law. The topic came up as the mother reminisce the elderly woman which winded down to the story of her daughter-in-law, the young widow.

As can be drawn from the narration of their story, Atipnao, a mother of two children, was widowed at a relatively young age, and it bonded her so close to her mother-in-law, who shared all her joys and sorrows. She treated the old lady as her own mother, and her mother-in-law treated her like her own too.

The young widow, enduring all the hardships, would do whatever she could to ensure that her mother-in-law is contended and happy.

On her death bed, it was said, the old lady called all her children and their respective families to come by her side. She then pronounced her final blessing. Thereafter, she asked her daughter-in-law, whom she loved so very dearly, to embrace her as she breathed her last. The villagers would all say and agreed, that the gesture was an expression of a deeply bonded love between the mother-in-law and Atipnao. A love as such was earned by the young widow with equal measure of love.

In a Tangkhul society, a daughter-in-law is considered as *matik kacha arihava* (an ideal daughter-in-law) if she treated her in-laws as her own parents and siblings. She is considered good if she took proper care of the parent-in-laws and treated them with respect. The logic behind this concept is that, a woman after marriage leaves behind her natal identity, habits, lifestyle, and food habits. She has to readjust her life in tune with her new identity, that is, with that of her husband's family. So, the daughter-in-law who could blend well with the in-laws is considered a glorified ideal. Case 14 mentioned above is one such example of an ideal *arihava.*

Another example characteristically reflecting the ideal of patriarchal and patrilineal values of the society instilled through sketches of character is narrated as follows.

Case 15: *One evening while visiting a family in the neighbourhood, I was invited to join them for dinner. As the table conversation begins, the father related the story of* ***Mr Asing****, who resides in the same locality. He stated that the burden the man had to shoulder as the eldest son after an untimely demise of his father. He had three brothers and a sister.*

Asing got married after the death of his father, and soon had to raise a family as a young father. He, being the eldest son in the family, has to look after his mother and younger siblings. The young father struggled for years to meet the needs of the family members on all fronts. He managed the family by taking up a small-time business, apart from his earnings from agricultural produces.

The young father did all he could, and invested his time and earnings on his younger brothers and sister. This, according to the narrator, is to ensure that he has shelter in times of trouble. This means that he can rely on them in future when difficult times come.

In later years, his younger brothers prospered in life. His immediate brother settled down in village, and extended all possible helps towards the construction of his new house. The two younger brothers, after completing their studies, settled down with a job and family. They did not settle in the village, but they were always ready to help whenever their elder brother is in need.

The authority of a man is associated with his status as the head of the family. One who can perform his duties and fulfil responsibilities of looking after his families is considered as masculine value - *mayarnao* (a man). This, a man accomplishes by exerting his authority and standing firm with an upright decision according to what the society sanctions. Case 15, is one such example of the quality of the eldest son.

The parents use characters of people as the cornerstone in teaching values to the children. The quality of those characters stands as examples to the younger ones. This way gender values are inculcated to children.

Children, by the age of six, spent their time outside their courtyard. Their activities involve school time, tuition hour, extra-curricular activities like song practice, sports, etc. and on Sundays, they attend Sunday school. Besides parental teachings, the children are now exposed to various factors that influence them in their process of internalising gender values. *Ngasotnao* (peer group), *worshim ngasotnao* (classmate) and *oja* (teachers) have their influence in moulding the child to his or her appropriate gender. The children also learn to mix with the opposite gender as well as with their own gender in the society which is not taught in the home environment. Children, at this stage become conscious of their own gender and gradually grasp the society's concept of what is considered good or bad to their gender.

13-18 YEARS

Individual come to terms with the new roles and physical changes and adjust with new phases in their lifecycle. By this stage, a child enters a new phase in their life. They attain puberty and become totally conscious of their biological differences. As they undergo a process of physical and mental changes, there is an awakening consciousness towards their gender role in the society. Gender values are reinforced by a person's change of status and their new place in the society.

The rite of passage among the Tangkhuls varies in different institutions. In their social institution, a boy is not considered an adult to represent the family until he is married. Among the girls, they are only given permanent status only when they become a legitimate *apareiva* (wife) to a man. In her father's house, she is only her *ava-wui naongalava* (father's daughter). Her status is not permanent in her father's house. Only after her marriage does she establish her permanent status as the *apareiva* (wife) of her husband and mother of her children. So, in case of unmarried men and women, they have to remain under the care of the oldest brother's family without established status.

In their political institution, women are not allowed to be members of the village political institution. A boy is inducted into the membership of this institution when they are considered matured enough to participate in the decision-making body, at about the age of 18.

In economic institution, they are counted as adult only when they attain the strength of an adult, that is by the age of 16 and this is applicable for both genders. Children below this age, for instance, do not enjoy the status of an adult labour wage.

In religious life, a person is inducted as members of the church after baptism. But there is no specific age-cut streamlined for such ceremonies. Usually, children get baptized by the age of 12 or 13 years or even later. Baptism marks the beginning of their service in their religious institution as active member. They are also allowed to partake in certain religious rituals like *prohowui phakachizat* (Lord's Supper), to participate in *chan khangazek* (Church assembly), youth service, etc.

As children mature and grow away from their parents in their behaviour, parents shift their attention from the previous role of looking after their physical needs to keeping strict vigil on the child's moral values. In the process of instilling this value, dichotomy is drawn between boys and girls in the way parents implement rules. A girl is advised to stay home after sunset with the exception of some social services and activities sanctioned by the society. The reason is partly due to the stigma of society, which they still adhere to, where girls who loiter around at unearthly hours are given a bad moral label and partly from the security perspective.

Boys of this age group are also bound by this advice but stringent rules are not imposed on them. For a boy of 16 years and above category, it is a conventional practice to go for fireside gathering (*meisum*) after dinner to girl's house in the village. It is this tradition that makes it impossible for the parents to impose strict rules on older boys of this age group. However, they are always advised to come back on time in order to avoid unnecessary interruption in their daily routine.

The process of socialisation, when viewed through the prism of gender, sheds new lights in almost every activity. In the course of investigating how children of this age group internalise gender values, the routine of a family in the neighbourhood every morning opened up new dimensions which became very relevant for my research. The incident that gave a spur to the investigation is given in the form of case study as follows.

Case 16: *In one of my usual morning rounds in the village, I came across an interesting incident which I observed minutely, and later discussed about it with an elderly onlooker in the neighbourhood.*

It was during the busy morning activities; I heard loud calls with an interval of loud bangs on the door. The mother and father would come to the doorstep of the son's room in rotation, to wake him up. They continued till he came out of the room. It is a tradition for the family to eat together. The parents, therefore, was bent on waking their son from his sleep and to join the rest of the family for a routine meal.

An elderly lady who lives next door remarked with a tint of humour that it is a meal time for the family, and the bell tolls— referring to the parent's repeated call of their son's name.

Ashang*, an 18-year-old boy, was home for summer break from his college. For him and all his mates, it was a usual affair to spend late nights for a leisurely gathering of meisum. The boy could not wake from his slumber in the morning, and this is the cause of all the drama which the neighbours witness every morning.*

The old lady told me that the mother would be in exasperating mood every morning, and would also be even heard saying that it is much easier to train a small boy. The mother, at times, murmured that it's now just a wishful thinking to see her son perform the morning duties.

The incident brought up so many research questions on whether it happens with other children of this age group or whether this practice cut across both genders. A pertinent question also lies with the impact of *meisum* in the larger spectrum of gender socialisation. The data illustrate disparities in the way parents impose discipline among the teenage children. The dichotomy, however, is deeply entrenched in the tradition which is structured by the gender setup of their culture. This portrayal is evident in the way girls are restraint within the walls of the house at night while sanctioning free movement of boys which they consider the norms of *meisum*. The differences are further illustrated in the role performance where girls who sit up late through the night for such gathering are not exempted from their morning chores. The incident was thus not a surmise of exceptional case but a fact of the socialisation process of adolescent children.

Children of this age group are now mentored to take responsibilities and meet the expectations appropriate to their gender. To emulate the role of a responsible father, boys are monitored to take firm and upright decision. Indecisiveness in men is scorned by the society. The usage of words "*Mayarnaona tashing eina matuilu*" which means men should speak decisively is a signifier of such value. Likewise, girls are expected to shoulder the responsibilities at home like the mother who bears the tasks as '*akhavaiva*' - wife of the *akhava* (head) of the household. The household management and culinary skills are taught to them so as to run the family smoothly when they are married. These gender values, treasured by the grandparents, still shows its firm grip even today which is evident in the way they reproduce in their daily lives.

Socialisation process, in the later adolescent stage, elicited a fresh chapter on understanding their status in kinship and marriage with the aim to create uniformity among the members of the society as they come to share values and attributes. Guidelines on rules of kinship, marriage (*ngalakhangakhot*) and incest (*shokhala and vakhalat*) are fed to them so that they do not deviate from the norms.

Kinship System

Children who have conceded the ritual of passage in various institutions of the society started to internalise the variegated functions of kinship. This aspect is one significant segment of gender socialisation which forms the core values as they take on roles of adulthood. The norms of convening a clan meeting comprising of all adult male members of the clan in case of misconduct by any member of the kin group, for instance, is taught to the adolescent boys so as to make them understand the responsibility and accountability of the members towards the kin group.

The value of solidarity among the kin group is also internalised by children as they participate in various activities of kin members. For instance, it is obligatory to lend a helping hand to relatives in case of any misfortune and difficult times. And in times of joy and celebration, all members of the kin group are invited to join the merriment. Case studies were taken up to examine the nature of how they uphold such solidarity.

Case 17: Mr. Apak *was seriously injured while chopping a tree in their forest plot. The news of the incident was relayed and spread within few minutes. That fateful afternoon, many people were seen hurrying towards the forest with a worried face. Those are his kin members and neighbours.*

The injured man was carried home. Immediately, a male relative rushed off to seek the doctor of the village health centre. That evening, in the victim's house, a score of visitors came to call on the family and lend their helping hands in every possible way.

For days and weeks, there were people visiting the house. The support from villagers came in different forms— money, material, physical and emotional helps. His recovery took months.

A significant observation made during this incident was the manifestation of the close-knit social fabric which contours their kinship system. Most of the people, who stayed up through night and day, assisted him to sit up, lie down or lean back, were lineage members ***(meiphung)*** *with the exception of few neighbours.*

I observed that the relatives, particularly women, came with big chickens, vegetables, sugar and tea leaves. While some would bring baskets of firewood, others would help the family with their agricultural activities in the field. The significance of what it is to be a part of a kin group could be seen in the way they help each other throughout the period of ailment.

The kin ties are reinforced by various ways of expressing that solidarity in difficult times and in times of celebration. The solidarity of the group is further strengthened by term of address among the members. Right from the time a child is born, he is taught to recognize her or his own group by teaching them the vocabulary of how to address a particular person. For instance, the child is taught to differentiate between the paternal aunts as '*ani +name*' and the maternal aunts as '*ava +name*' like *anilung* or *avalung*. As they learn these terminologies, they are taught to respect elders too, through their usage of kinship terminologies. The children are always taught never to address elders by their names without the proper prefix. For instance, the prefixes *amei/achon* (elder brother/sister) or *ani/awo* (aunt/ uncle) are terms of respect to elders. These way children are taught to differentiate between the male and female kin.

A well-regulated pattern of behaviour among the kin members is another factor strengthening kin ties. The practice of *chonlan* (*chon* from *kashan kachon* meaning clothes and *lan* from *khalan* implies present or gift) is one such practice of acknowledging their kin relations. Such gifts in the form of shawls and lower garments are given by women on occasions like *shakaza (*wedding), *maran kasa* (merit feast), *kathi kasar* (death ceremony), *thisham* (death anniversary), *phanit* (festivals), etc. As reciprocal token of their love, men slaughter a pig, a cow or buffalo for the married sisters and aunts.

Case 18: *On the occasion of the Church centenary celebration in the village,* **Mrs Aning** *returned to her parent's home after many years. She had not visited her birthplace since her marriage. It was a memorable visit for the woman as the place un-wrapped fond reminiscence of her childhood in the village. "It feels like I am travelling back to the old days with a carefree spirit," she recalled.*

For the woman, it was one of her happiest times to relive her memories at parental home— as their daughter and a native of the village.

In our conversation, she recalled how her friends and herself as kids were bullied and got their share of punishments, in school and at home. She also fondly remembered the moment when she exchanged her pen with that of her brother, and her proud excitement to brag about it to all her friends. Since her childhood days, she had a strong attachment with her elder brothers and that it gave her a great sense of pride whenever she was treated with some endearments.

The ceremony of send-off blessing on the eve of her wedding, for this woman, was so memorable as she presented the shawls to all her brothers and her parents as a token of love. It was followed by gifts which she proudly took it to her husband's home.

She is a mother of four children, and resides in the district headquarters. From time to time, her brothers would come from the village and stay with them. The visits as such were eagerly awaited by her children, as they also share a close attachment as maternal uncles. The children would always look forward to the bedtime stories and jokes, which their uncles were ever ready to entertain them with.

The visit of Aning and her children during this occasion of their Church programme was marked by gifting of shawl to her brother and a wrap-around (lower garment) for his wife. The symbolic expression of the reciprocal ties could be read through slaughtering of a pig to mark her arrival. Even after she was married and moved away to other place, she continued to express the bliss of sharing such love and ties with her brothers.

The case study elicited a fresh understanding on the maternal kin ties where children too are dynamic participants. Besides maintaining a strong bond among the paternal kin, that is primarily patrilineal, the close knit ties with the maternal relations cannot be overlooked. There always exist a special bond between the children and the maternal uncle. This relationship developed through their mother who cared so much for her brother. The term '*varei*' is used for the eldest maternal uncle who plays an important role in the life of the sister's children and takes the role of a guardian. In return, the children are taught to respect him, whose love and affection is counted as the greatest blessing.

The characteristic preponderance of patriliny, however, limits the maternal ties to a generation. The kinship tie is closer on the maternal side only during the mother's lifetime. With the death of the mother, this bond gradually loses its vibrancy. In this regard, there is a saying which goes –

"Ngalarava thotkhamanga, kha mayarawuiya mithot peida mashimanlui mana".

This literally means that maternal kinship last only for a generation whereas, paternal kinship is a long-lasting social bond. Hence, whatever the relationship may be, the maternal bond cannot surpass the paternal bond in this patrilineal society. A man who ignores his allegiance towards his paternal kin is considered a socially insensible person.

The paradigm shift of the economy with the corresponding changes in other aspects of their culture has resulted to occupational relocation, and thereby, bringing changes in their tradition of daily courtesy calls among the kin members. Frequent visits and regular exchange of farm produces has become a thing of the past among many kin members. To make a comparative study of the changes in this aspect, an account given by some elderly women may be referred here. This case study was recorded when I sat with them one Sunday afternoon.

Case 19: *The common form of greeting among the Tangkhuls, when they meet or passed by each other, comes in a ubiquitous way— Maphazahaira (Have you had your meal?), Khihan shai khala? (What dish did you have?).*

When the three aged women sat together, their conversation began with an enquiry on the main dish of the meal. One would complain about the food; the other blamed it on her loss of appetite, while the other woman rued, "How I wish I had those strong teeth to grind and munch dry meat delicacies." They shifted their topic, after wishful murmurings, on smoked meat prepared by ***Anong***— *the oldest lady among them. Her two friends expressed their cravings and wishes to go back in time to relish them.*

Of the three women, Anong used to shoulder greater responsibilities in childcare and in the fields. Her friends talked about the burdens she faced as her husband was an avid hunter, who would frequently be away from home. A smart hunter that he was, the man would never come home without a catch. Whenever Anong's husband returned from hunting, he would invite relatives to come over and collect their share. He was very generous and ensured that all the kin members and the neighbours receive a share of meat.

With the surplus meat, Anong would smoke them meticulously and store in baskets atop the mantle. So, neighbours and relatives would come over asking for her smoked meat when their menu is not appetizing. They would then always return their generosity by extending helping hands in their agricultural works and other activities.

In our interactions, I also learnt that the women shared whatever dishes they prepared every meal and all kinds of preserved food items. Even in their aging days, they continued to spend Sunday afternoons together and endeared themselves by sharing the traditional snacks prepared at their respective kitchen. These women looked at the current scene of kin ties with critical candour. As one of them chipped in, "Not long ago, sharing precedes selling"— which is indicative of the corresponding changes of economy and social ties that have come about.

The feature depicted here so eloquently is the reinforcement of kin ties through exchange of things and visits. A comparative study of case 18 and 19 shows that changes have come about in the way kin ties are strengthened through varying practices. The aged people could not come to terms with the widening gap among the kin members and considered the current practices as dismal scene. The contemporary scene of kin ties is depicted in case 18 in which the physical distance is covered with occasional meetings and sharing. This shows that the ties are not severed but continuity is maintained through other forms as time and situation demands.

Gender relations are also expressed through usage of kinship terms. Most spouses who come under the purview of the present study belong to the younger generation. The couples address one another by their names or by adding the prefix *amei,* meaning older men or elder brother (older men being more appropriate in the context). A wife addresses her husband, for instance, whose name is *Ashang* as *Amei-shang* (prefix+name). A husband, on the other hand, addresses his wife by her name without any prefix. The prefix is usually added as a term of respect. The term of respect is only added in addressing the husband and not vice versa. In the past, there was certain avoidance of names for certain people. This difference is evident in the way the aged spouse addresses one another with their children's names as *Ashang-shava or Ashang-shavā,* which means *Ashang's* mother or father. They maintain teknonymy while addressing each other.

Kinship term is rather rigid among the siblings. The younger ones are not supposed to address elders by their names. Likewise, older ones address them with proper prefix. For instance, the eldest kin of both genders were addressed as *achon* or *amei* without their names. The others are addressed as *amei + name* or *achon + name.* The younger ones are addressed as

Apa - sister to younger brother,

ikatuiva - sister to younger sister,

izarra - brother to younger sister, and

ikato - brother to younger brother.

The asymmetrical gender relations in kinship system of the Tangkhuls are expressed in diverse ways. Though traces of changes have taken various aspects of their tradition to different courses, the rudiments of patriliny and patriarchy continue to find its ways, the evidence of which is unraveled in varied vistas of gender socialisation.

Marriage: A study on kinship system of the Tangkhul would be incomplete without exploring on another aspect of their social unit - marriage institution. As legible through the social fabric of human society, kinship network starts from the family, which originates from the union of two people. As such, it becomes inevitable to analyze the marriage system contiguous with their kinship structure.

Marriage is a significant subject of discussion in gender socialisation as it foregrounds a strong note of gendered perspective in later stage of adolescent life. The institution of marriage is one of the means of social control through which members of the society behave within the approved social sanctions and refrains from being promiscuous. The rules of whom to marry and what is incest or taboo are imbibed through the teaching of parents and elders.

The Tangkhul society maintains strict rules of clan exogamy as they believe that they come from the same genealogical descent. So, a child is taught to refrain from such incestuous act. Violation of such rules is known as *'shokhala'*, which is literally interpreted as "upside down," meaning 'incest'. Another taboo regarding marriage is prohibition of union between a man's son and his sister's daughter, which is known as *'vakhalat,'* meaning 'returning to the maternal uncle.' In the past, couples who violate these rules were punished with expulsion from the clan and the village.

The society still adheres to the belief that incestuous acts bring curse on their lives. Such unions are stigmatised by the society and bar them from assuming any social position. Till today, it is found that such marriages are very rare. The act of *shokhala* and *vakhalat* is viewed upon with ignominy by the society. Parents, as such, not only teach their children not to deviate from the norms of marriage but monitor them under strict vigil.

Apart from what is considered as incest, the Tangkhuls have a preferential type of marriage known as *pam* marriage. This is a type of cross cousin's marriage where a sister's son is allowed to marry the maternal uncle's daughter. It is a form of taking her aunt's place on the part of the daughter. This type of marriage is favoured with the belief that such marriage brings closer ties among the kin group and to ease adjustment problems. Such marriage was usually arranged by families in the past though younger generations today have swerved from such practices.

Marriage, in most cases, is the outcome of youthful courtship which however ensues with the approval of their parents. Based on what is and what is not sanctioned by the customary laws of marriage, parents always teach their children to keep away from intimate association with whom they cannot marry. In this regard, parents interfere in the children's choice of friendship irrespective of gender.

There is no parental objection in sharing friendly company between the sexes. The community-based activities evidently show participation of boys and girls in the same platform in most occasions. However, the recurrent theme of parents' advice is to maintain restraints in physical proximity between the sexes not even in playful situation. The reason for such restriction is not far to seek as their saying unveils:

Meili ngareo akha ngator,

Mayarnaoli ngareo akha naovai,

(If you play with fire, you get scalded;

if you play with men, you get conceived.)

Teachings on physical proximity come with strict restriction particularly for girls. This is eloquently depicted through the sayings. The reality hidden under the heap of this statement is apparent of the dichotomy between women and men. The image of women getting pregnant without proper formalities of marriage is looked upon with askance and the credence of stigma is relatively more compared to that of men.

Against the background of gender socialisation, teaching on choosing life partner assumes a significant subject in the later adolescent stage. There are certain qualities which are widely acknowledged as consensus standards over the prerequisite or selection of partner. In this context, the consensus standards may be defined by aspects like economy, equation in the family, personal qualities, biological antecedents, religion, ethnic preference and education. In this regard, parents as well as children of this age group were interviewed.

Marriage outside the village was very rare in the past. The village was the epicenter of their universe as they have no contact with the outside world. With the changes that have come about in various aspects of their life, a path breaker in the tradition of marriage is intermarriage which has become very prevalent in the contemporary Tangkhul society. In the context of the present discussion, intermarriage denotes marrying someone outside the village boundary and outside the tribe. However, older generations always advise to choose life partner within the village community or from the neighbouring villages that shares similar practices to avoid adjustment hitches. The trend however shows diversion from the traditional norm as there are many cases of intermarriage today which is indicative of the fact that the deeply entrenched belief to such value has started breaking from the norm.

They strongly believe in the unity of a family by sharing the same faith or religion. The whole population of the village follows Christianity. They take serious note of this factor when it comes to marriage. There are some cases of women marrying outside their belief system. But, a man taking in a non-Christian wife is non-existent. If this kind of marriage happened, they will accept her only after her conversion. A greater restriction is emphasised on men which is an expression of their patriliny.

Genealogical factor is one aspect which is given a serious thought in selection of life partner among the Tangkhuls. The factor is not restricted only to the mental and physical disability, but is inclusive of factors like *mirai kakaza, khangayei* and other genetic diseases. *Mirai kakaza*, according to the belief of the Tangkhuls, may be defined as sadistic possession of a person by the spirit of another person. *Khangayei* is a term used to refer to human being transformed into animal form. Hereditary diseases like spastic, skin diseases, mentally unsound, kleptomania, tuberculosis etc. are taken into consideration. The maxim of the Tangkhuls, *"Makathar katongava pheotapai serra kha asheeli pakahai kazatva mapheoluipai mana"* speaks it all. It literally means that 'one can wash off anything that is dirty but disease that is in the blood (the concept of blood here is synonymous with genetic traits) cannot be cleansed'.

In the backdrop of HIV/AIDS pandemic, another important factor in selection of life partner is the emphasis on the morality of a person. The society has lost many lives due to substance abuse and HIV/AIDS. This led them to stress on a person's history as an important criterion in selecting a partner. Certain personal qualities like alcoholism, drug abuse and behavioural conduct of a person are seriously taken into consideration irrespective of gender.

In choosing a partner, economic status of a family is also considered as a determining factor. This is mostly applicable in case of choosing a son-in-law by parents. The logic behind this is that parents want to send their daughter to an economically stable family so as to ease her from economic burden. Because, a girl after her marriage becomes a permanent member of the husband's family and manages the economy of the family as *akhavaiva.*

Gender equation of the family too is one unique factor in the selection of partners. The term denotes the number of siblings a person has in the family. The number of male siblings is given pivotal importance though the female siblings are considered as additional criteria. A family with many sons is considered a good family which is termed as *"chinao khamathashi"* ('*chinao*' literally means sibling and '*khamathashi*' means good). The relativity of the concept is synonymous with the concept of *'mak chinao khamatha,'* which means good numbers of brother in-laws from the security point of view. This has its derivatives from the practices of maintaining reciprocal ties among the in–laws in which they lend a helping hand to each other in times of misfortune, trouble, or other circumstances.

Considering the criteria of partner, engagement proceeds with the proposal from the boy's family. A middle person, usually a female relative known as *ngala hangsang khamiva*, is entrusted with the task of meeting the girl's parents and asks for their daughter's hand in marriage. If the proposal is acceptable to both the parties, then a date is fixed for the betrothal. In the past, omens were consulted before they fix the schedule to predict whether the union of the couple is favourable. If the omen is positive, they go ahead with the betrothal; if not, the engagement was cancelled. However, the practice of consulting omens has now lost its relevance today.

A betrothal ceremony is customarily conducted at the girl's house with members of the two families including both men and women, besides all the elder members of the *meiphung*. Friends of the girl and the boy may also be invited to the occasion. Only male members of the two families participate in the formality though women may attend but refrain from participation in the discussion. On this occasion, the bride's family must know the share of properties for the groom, both movable and immovable. This is done for security of the couple and especially for the daughter.

In the past, a spade and a rupee were given to the bride's family as a significant token of good wishes and biding that the couple have a lasting and fruitful marriage. The spade signifies fruitful life, and the coin signifies precious union and lasting relationship. Today, such practices, however, have lost its significance. The ritual of '*chonlan*' *(*shawl presentation) still occupies a significant practice in which the bride gives shawl to the groom on the betrothal ceremony to signify respect, love and honour between the couple. A feast is an indispensable part of the event.

A pig slaughtered for the occasion is given to the groom's family. This is known as '*paiyansa*', meaning 'declaration meat'. The meat is distributed to all the relatives and *meiphung.* The groom's family formally hands over certain amount of money to the bride's family as part of contribution for expenses towards wedding preparations.

The nuptial preparation calls for both financial and material arrangement. *Kachon* (shawls) and *kashan* (lower wrap-around garment) are prepared by both the families for the wedding. All kin women extend their help in weaving. Men, on the other hand, get ready with the woods for fuel and make arrangements with the animals to be slaughtered for the occasion.

On the eve of the ceremony, a send-off party is held at the bride's residence to bid farewell from her natal home. The ceremony includes a formal gathering of guests and invitees, who are mostly of kin members, relatives, and friends. Some people even give a feast for the whole village community. The bride gives away shawls and lower wrap-around garment (*kashan*) to her family members as gifts to remember her by. She receives blessing from the family and from the *varei* (eldest maternal uncle). Relatives, friends and family attend the occasion with their share of contribution known as *shimlam.*

A wedding ceremony is held in the church solemnised by a pastor, who declares their union in marriage. The groom then takes the bride home ceremoniously in the best of tradition. However, before she enters the threshold of the groom, the gifts from her parental home are delivered but with a charge for the delivery group who are women of the clan. These women would perform raillery as they teasingly mock the bride's family through folk songs threatening them that they would take the bride back if they do not get a good share, which is normally given in the form of money.

The entrance of the bride into her new home is marked with a welcoming ceremony from the womenfolk of the groom's family. She, then, distributes shawls to the groom's family along with kitchen wares to all sister-in-laws – *yorla* to mark her entry into the family. This ceremony is followed by a feast which is usually attended by all the villagers and invitees. However, all these are done according to the capacities of the family's economic condition.

Another type of wedding is home marriage, which usually takes place in case of remarriage on either side of the party. The pastor is invited in the house of the groom to perform the necessary ceremony at home. Such ceremony is attended only by close relatives and clan members. Formalities of engagement are not necessarily imposed for such marriage and the wedding may take place within a short period of time.

There is another type of marriage, which is also very common among the people, and that is the case of elopement. The reasons for such marriages are variegated, which in most instances are associated with conflict between personal choice and that of the elders or out of complicated issues, which render their union unsuitable for conventional wedding. Some case studies are as under.

Case 20: *An informant of my research once blatantly expressed his disagreement against the mindset of the older generation for their stubborn stand on how their children should choose a life partner. His argument was that the person should decide by himself or herself in choosing a partner, instead of taking other's suggestion. His argument exuded from his own bitter experience that forced him to elope with the girl of his choice.*

Mr and Mrs Aleng had been childhood friends. As they grew up their friendship blossomed to love relationship. Their efforts to get their parents' consent, however, did not yield a favourable result. The girl's parents were against their courtship due to the boy's economic background. For some years they tried their best to convince the girl's parents, but to no avail. The girl's family came up with an arrangement of sending her away for further studies. This plan was made with an intention to separate them by distance. On learning the plan, they finally eloped without the consent of the girl's parents.

It was this experience that had made him ridicule the placid acceptance of elders to economic criteria, which indeed forced him to flout the conventional practice of wedding. On the part of his wife, she rejected the easy submissive role of a daughter her parents expected of her to play with regard to the choice of marital partner.

Case 21: *A comprehensive insight on the reasons of deviating from the conventional norm can be seen through the story of* ***Mrs Alungla****, whose case is one of the most frequent characteristics of my studies. She was merely 16 years when she got married. It was not a conscious choice for her, but compelled by situation. She got impregnated by her boyfriend when she was a tenth standard student. For three months, she managed to conceal her pregnancy from everyone except her boyfriend, with whom she had tried to find all possible ways to solve the problem. In spite of her best effort to hide it from her mother, she could not get away with an excuse from her mother's prying eyes and inquisitive mind. Not knowing what to decide and how to tackle the problem, she confessed to her mother.*

On learning the realities of her daughter and the predicament that it has put her in, the mother was in deep distraught and filled with anger. Her mother took some time to take a call on the situation. Few days later, her mother had something in mind and decided to have audience with the boy. She then insisted that both of them to get eloped before her father finds out. The girl and the boy found the mother's proposal quite acceptable, while fully comprehending the outcome of defying the wish of her father.

Thus, they eloped as suggested by the girl's mother— without the knowledge of the father. Much against the dreams of her younger days of having a big wedding and blessings from her parents, she left her natal home and thus became a mother.

Divergent strands from the conventional norm could be seen in such cases of marriage. In the first case, it is apparent that they could not get the approval of the parents; while in the second case, it happened by compulsion due to pregnancy. In many cases, the spouse falls short of certain prerequisite stated earlier which led to opposition from parents on either side. In few rare cases, it is caused by breach of marriage laws like *shokhala* or *vakhalat*.

Situating the case studies against the cultural context to which the individuals are always reacting and adjusting to, it is clear that they uphold the former type of marriage ceremony while the latter is accepted but with askance. The fact is not far to seek as in the case of the former type, they take up the ceremony with acceptance of both the families; whereas in the latter, the union of the couple posits the chances of non-acceptance from the family members for which such incident happened. The consequences may not be cordial for the girl if she becomes an unwelcomed member in the conjugal house which may not be the case with man. It is because women are subsumed with the identity of men and not vice versa which is indicative of patriliny.

Marriage through elopement remains traditionally unrecognised until it is legitimized through the process of *vahem*. The performance of this ceremony marks the acknowledgement of the couple as husband and wife, which calls for participation of both the families. Soon after the couple enter the threshold of the man, an elderly man of the lineage or family is sent to inform the girl's parents about the elopement. From then on, preparations are made for a ceremony known as *vahem*. On the fixed day, the family along with the lineage members of the man goes to the woman's house with a livestock for the occasion, which may be in the form of a pig (*hok*) or buffalo (*silui*) for the occasion. Shawls (*kachon*) are gifted to the parents, siblings and relatives to mark her departure from the parental home. The woman's family, on the other hand, would enquire the details of the son's share in their family immovable assets like house, forest land, paddy fields, etc. The tradition is rooted in the legal principle of assuring security of the daughter. After all the formalities are performed, the ceremony is concluded with a feast signifying the acknowledgement of their union and marking the beginning of the family ties between the two families.

Thereafter, the girl's family makes arrangement for presentation ceremony known as *Shaksakhami* (literally meaning 'pack up'). This ceremony is hosted by the women's family with a feast where the daughter is sent away from the natal home to her husband's house with her share, usually in the form of movable property like household wares, jewelleries, etc. This ritual, indeed, is a matter of pride for the woman as it signifies that she did not enter the husband's house empty handed. It also underlines the fact that she has a family whom she may repose her trust, reciprocate with love and who can protect her. Though women partake in such ceremonies, they are not allowed to participate in discussion and decision-making.

Internalisation of customary laws on the whole process of engagement, marriage ceremony, or customary rules and practices pertaining to elopement and rule of heredity, taught to the adolescent comes with gendered conditions. The overall sketch outlines the patriarchal and patrilineal values of the society. The send-off blessing ceremony, for instance, is implicative of the patrilineal continuity. The entrance of the bride to the threshold of the groom is again symbolic of her change of identity and status – from a daughter of her father to a wife of her husband. The ceremony of *vahem*, on the other hand, signifies the patriarchal nature of the society where men perform the formalities without women's participation in discussion and decision-making. The internalisation process thus comes with gendered manual as they take on their gender role as adults of the society.

Side by side with the teachings of the customary practices, children at their adolescent stage exhibit significant gendered behaviour in more ways than one. Gendered division of labour in the family, for instance, becomes very apparent. There is a degree of socialisation along the same sex line between parent and children as well. Mother-daughter relationship is more intense than father-daughter relationship. Stringent surveillance imposed on girls, at this stage, may be regarded as one factor binding them to take up more chores within the vicinity of their home like weaving, cleaning, washing, etc. Boys, on the other hand, are left to run errands outside their home.

Analysis on the socialisation of older children among the third age group (13–18 years) brings out a substantial marker of gender. Children move out from home after they pass their class tenth examination either to pursue higher studies or to take up other vocation. In order to examine the role of parents on the choice of the children's profession through the lens of gender socialisation, samples of fifteen families (five each from three income groups) were collected, which are presented in the following tables.

Table 11. Occupational Gender Status of Low Income Group

Sample Families	Clan	Income group	No. of Children*	Occupation of children**	
				Girls	Boys
Family 1	Khamrang	Low	2	Class x (Local/ Govt)	Class xii (outside)
Family 2	Ruivah	Low	2	Low-cost vocational training (outside)	Class xi (outside)
Family 3	Muivah	Low	3	(i) Dropped studies after class x (iii) Class viii (local/Govt.)	(ii) Class x (Local/Govt.)
Family 4	Rungsung	Low	3	(i) Work as helper (outside) (ii) Helps the parents at home	(iii) Class vii (local/Govt.)
Family 5	Shimrang	Low	2	(ii) Stay with parents	(i) Part time job (outside)

Source: Fieldwork.

Table 12. Occupational Gender Status of Moderate Income Group

Sample Family	Clan	Income group	No. of children	Occupation of children	
				Girls	Boys
Family 1	Ruivah	Moderate	3	(i) Short-term Training(outside) (iii) Class viii (Local/govt. school)	(ii) Class x (outside)
Family 2	Muivah	- do -	3	(ii) Class ix (local/govt.) (iii) Class viii (local/govt)	(i) Class xi (outside)
Family 3	Phungshok	- do -	2	(i) Class x (local govt)	(ii) Class viii (local/private)
Family 4	Ronra Shimray	- do -	2	(i) Nursing (outside)	(ii) Class xii (outside)
Family 5	Ruivah	- do -	2	(i) Part time job (outside)	(ii) Class x (outside)

Source: Fieldwork.

Table 13. Occupational Gender Status of High Income Group

Sample Family	Clan	Income Group	No. of Children	Occupation/Status of children	
				Girls	Boys
Family 1	Muivah	High	2	(i) Class xii (outside)	(ii) Class xi (outside)
Family 2	Khamrang	- do -	3	(ii) Class xi (Outside) (iii) Class ix (local/ Private)	(i) BCA (outside)
Family 3	R. Shimray	- do -	2	(i) Class x (local/ private)	(ii) Class viii (local/private)
Family 4	Shimrang	- do -	2	(ii) Class xi (outside)	(i) Profnl.Course (outside)
Family 5	Rungsung	- do -	2	(ii) Class xi (outside)	(i) Class xii (outside)

Source: Fieldwork

* Number of children in the table denotes only the number of children within the age group between 13–18 years in the family.

** In the occupation/status column:

i, ii, iii = children according to their age

Local= in the village

Outside = outside the village

Private = Private school (more expensive)

Govt = Government school (low-cost)

The tables represent data of three income groups. Limitations, among the low-income group, are set by economic constraint where parents and children are not in the position to make the choice according to what they like or on what they are good at. It rather becomes an issue of livelihood. Yet in some other cases, the situation of preferences sets in as they are not economically equipped to let the children pursue what they want. They either have to send the children outside the village to work somewhere for livelihood or they have to choose among the children to pursue their studies. This is when patrilineal values raise its head as it always is on the valued side of the ledger.

The moderate-income group comparatively fare better in this regard. Children of this group enjoy better opportunities and the display of gender disparity is less significant as compared to the low-income group. However, the evidence of disparity could not be ignored when the number of children is large. The same trend of preferential scheme is apparent in this case as well, though it presents here with a different facade. In its noteworthy outline, the preference comes with the question of whom to send to private school or government sponsored school or for long-term professional course and short-term vocational training though all children get the opportunity to pursue their studies. In the end, the answer is not far to seek with patriliny trailing behind in whatever they decide.

The high-income group display contrasting picture as far as the case under the discussion is concerned. Parents are much at liberty to support their children and children have ample freedom to pursue what they want. This however should not be taken at face value as parents always show more concern towards boys with the perception that they should be able to stand on their own feet with their head held high as a man when they grow up. The notion evidently depicts what a man should be as a patriarch in the Tangkhul society.

The above analysis is the discussion on the children of the three income groups. The picture may however change in the long run when they cross these age groups. For instance, equal choice and equal share given to the children during this period may be altered when they reach older stage of their life.

The above discussions are some of the significant observations of how gender values are internalised by children. Summative analysis shows that parental teachings rooted in the conventional traditions of the society, and it forms the fundamental base that influenced the young inquisitive minds of children. Children also learn gender values through observation and imitation. Thus, gender values are inculcated in an overt and covert ways.

It is also observed that patriarchal values of the society play a vital role in gender socialisation. These values are indelibly infused which is manifested through verbal and non-verbal performance. Certain occasions like *naoyan, naoming kaphok,* courtship, and marriage ceremony are instances of such manifestations.

Gender socialisation, thus, begins literally from birth. This process conditions a boy and a girl into two categories which function together in a culture. However, parents who believe they give equal treatment to boys and girls tend to produce different responses.

However, socialisation is a process in the evolution of any society which is not static. So, what one observes today may be the outcome of the changes that have come about from yesteryears and it may change over a period of time. Different agents contribute to the progress of socialisation will be discussed in the next chapter.

Chapter - IV

Continuity and Change in Gender Socialisation

Roles, functions and responsibilities each gender traditionally held are expressive of gender relations within that society. The relations are passed on from one generation to another through socialisation process. It is impossible to understand the socialisation process without examining the agents through which gender operates in sustaining the continuity. In a similar way, it is equally necessary to examine the changes in order to understand how it stands today without having a perspective on how it was in the past. The discussion here would therefore focus on how change and continuity are outlined through the agents of socialisation.

The agents of socialisation are structured group or context within which significant process of socialisation occurs. In the Tangkhul society, the *shimkhur* (family) is the principle socialising agent of the child during infancy. The other influences become significant agents as the child grows up which include *yarnao* (peers), *worshim* (schools), *dharma* (religion) and mass media. The continuity and changes of gender relations are thus made visible through these agents.

The chapter here analyses different agents of gender socialisation as factors responsible for both continuity and change in gender relations. In the process of considering what has changed and what is being continued, the present agents are outlined against the background of what agents played identical role in the past.

1. Socialisation within the family

The first imprint of gender to the infant is given by the family members. Family, as agents of socialisation, inculcates the notion of what masculinity or femininity is through verbal and non-verbal clues. Among the Tangkhuls, the family (*shimkhur*) consists of father (*ava*), mother (*ava*), children (*naongara*), grandparents - grandmother *(ayi)* and grandfather (*awo*), and sometime, unmarried siblings of the father; aunts (*ani*) and *avakato* (uncles). Each member, consciously and unconsciously, act as agents of gender socialisation, the influence of whose role is based on their status in the family.

***Ava* (Mother):** The concept of child-rearing for a mother starts even before a child is born. According to their beliefs, a pregnant woman should restraints herself from visiting certain places which is considered as *ngalei kharar* (haunted place) and should stay indoor after sunset lest a malevolent spirit may possess her. She also refrains herself from eating certain food as mentioned in Chapter III. The concept itself symbolises the life force a mother represents. She takes the centre-stage in the process of socialisation as she takes the prelude of the child's initial periods and continues to play the pivotal role throughout the childhood stages and beyond.

The recurrent theme of gender attributes could be read from all things with which a mother associates with the baby. The tailoring of gender tag to a child, for instance, is evident in the gender-typed clothes and the gender-specific pet names a mother uses like *achonkharar* (to the eldest daughter), *lateophy* (to a daughter with small physiological structure), *paishonao* (to a youngest daughter) etc. to a girl child or *ameikharar* (to the eldest son), *atao* (to younger son), etc. to a boy child. Gendering could be read even in the way a mother soothes the baby and through gender typed toys she provides.

A mother is the first person to teach gender oriented configuration to the child. The portraiture of her role in training the child to meet the social expectations is noticeable from how a mother reprimands her son "*mayarnaona ning khani machipaimana*," which literally means, 'a man cannot be indecisive'. This symbolically denotes the perpetuation of masculine value of man as the decision maker. The juxtaposition of gender values is apparent in the teaching "*ngalanaona malung nimlu*", which indicates 'a girl should possess a soft temperament' attributing to the feminine value of maintaining herself a graceful nature. The role of the mother as an important agent of socialisation on gender values is supplemented with gendered role assignment to the children.

For a girl child, she plays a definitive role in imparting gendered activities, duties, nurturing maternal role and responsibilities associated with feminine characteristics. She internalises the feminine skills starting from the minor duties to facing the task of managing a household. The influence of the mother is considered as the model to her daughter and this is the reason that the daughters are looked upon as the personification of the mother. The truism of the concept is expressed with a saying which goes,

"Ngala hui akha avali huire falu"

Literally, it says 'if you woo a girl, know her mother first' — a phrase metaphorically suggestive of the fact that daughters are the reflections of their mother.

The attainment of puberty initiates a girl to the beginning of womanhood where the mother takes the responsibility of teaching the daughters on moral values. Besides assuming the role of a teacher, a mother shoulders the responsibility of monitoring the behaviour and movements of the daughter to save ignominy from the judgmental eyes of the society.

A mother also acts as mediator between the husband and children. The norm of the society has this tradition where children, especially adolescent, are emotionally more attached to the mother. So, the issue which they could not discuss directly to the father is conveyed by the mother that fits her to the role of a mediator. Her role is also true vice-versa when the message has to be cut across from father to the children.

***Ava* (Father):** The traditional practice of the society sanctions limited role to a father till the age of two. This is so as the mother and grandmother take the role of nurturing the small child in their hands. It will however be wrong to assume a non-participatory image of the father at this stage. The occasional role of babysitting, indeed, is a frequent scene in the field. It is also a routine for the father to take the small child who had just started to walk and talk to tag along with him for a stroll or visit to the neighbours.

The pivotal role of the father in gender socialisation shows prominence with children attaining the age of five. With children of this age group, he stands as the epitome of the values associated with men in their cultural set up. For his children, the concept of what masculinity means is personified in the totality of the father. The role of the father to his son is manifested through his teachings on decision-making and on the authority vested in him as the head of the family.

The father instills the penchant for masculine traits, teaching his sons gendered role in the division of labour. He takes the growing boy in his hand as he teaches duties and responsibilities appropriate for a man. The masculine skills of handling household implement for mending and repairing works are trained by the father. A young boy tags along with the father to the paddy fields to check the water outlets. At other times, he would follow him to the *jhum* fields to clear the bushes or accompany him to chop wood for fuel.

The grandparents - ***awo*** (grandfather) and ***ayi*** **(**grandmother) play a significant role in the life of a growing child. During infancy, children spent most of their time with the grandmother. She is the substitute of the mother and assumes her role whenever the mother is away for work. She plays a key role in gender socialisation and has been an agent who had perpetuated gender values over the years. In the village, the grandmothers mostly look after two to three children, and sometimes, even more. This is so as her stay at home acts as daycare center for children of the neighbourhood. Her duties of looking after these children is associated with verbal feedings of gender specific values and through actions as she feeds them, change their diapers and clothes.

The scene of a grandfather taking a walk, while humming a folk lullaby as he lovingly cuddles a small child carried on his back with warm shawl along the yard of the neighbourhood, is a common sight. This in itself is a tangible expression of the *awo's* role in the life of grandchildren during the stage of childhood. There is a saying among the Tangkhuls, which goes—

"Awo ngarava naoli langmeida ara ngarali phungmeiya"

(The grandfathers carry their grandchildren more than their own children)

The act as such is the testimony of their love for the grandchildren. However, his role is limited during infancy and early childhood as the grandmother or the mother takes major responsibilities of nurturing like feeding, changing clothes and diapers, and other nursing cares.

By the time the child grows older, the grandparents assume an advisory role as they begin teaching the children through narration of folktales and customary laws and practices. The influence through this role is fundamental in shaping gendered characteristics as every story and every customary law is a way of how people streamline gender values of each sexes.

Older siblings, *achon* (elder sister), ***amei*** (elder brother): In the milieu of a family, the older siblings, as an agent of socialisation, influence the *apanao* (a term of address used by a girl to the younger brother), *akatuiva* (a girl to a younger sister), *azarva* (a boy to a younger sister), *akato* (a boy to a younger brother). The younger child learns to identify his or her sex with his siblings and gradually learns to fit into their gender status through them. They are the first group of children with whom the child learns to socialise in a group.

Role of the older siblings in socialisation are immense as one would witness the explicit expression in the way they carry the younger ones around even in their play. Unlike the urban scene, the older siblings, however young they may be, learn to carry the infant on their back and take responsibility of looking after them when the mother is away for work or the grandmother is busy with other duties at home.

By the age of three, a child joins in the play session of the older siblings in their own imaginary world known as *thangthang*. The older children allocate gender roles to each person and the scene demonstrates the role of an adult men and women. They emulate the roles as assigned according to their gendered division of labour which becomes role learning and eventually role performance in real life in the later stage.

As they grow up the younger ones take on the gendered behaviour of their older siblings. The children follow the older ones in gender specific games in which the younger boys follow older boys and vice versa. The scene of playing marble of an older boy teaming up with his younger brother against brothers of the neighbourhood or a team of sisters against another sisters' team in the game of five stones (*kotla*) is a common sight which is a tangible expression of the role of older siblings as agents of gender socialisation.

***Ani/Avagato* (Paternal Aunt and Uncle), *Avakatui/Awo* (Maternal Aunt and Uncle):** The principles of gender could also be heard in the voices of aunts and uncles. Like other members of the family, aunts and uncles give gender stereotyped treatment to their nieces and nephews. They give verbal and non-verbal clues to children in identifying their place in the society.

The aunts, like that of the mother and grandmother, influence children as they take on maternal role. Right from the birth of a child, she actively involves herself in childcare. Aunts mostly take care of the older ones when the mother could no longer take care of them. The older children usually sleep with their *ani* as younger ones come along.

Young boys spend time with the uncles and copy his behaviour and roles. A paternal uncle is one person whom boys placed as a model in the process of growing up. A maternal uncle, on the other hand is one person with whom children look up with honour and share a special bond through the mother and his advice is considered valuable. Though the role of uncles is limited in childcare, their role in later stage of childhood is evident in role learning and giving proper guidance to children.

The most frequent faces to an infant are the *ava* (mother), *ani* (aunt) and *ayi* (grandmother). These women of the family endear the infant with stereotyped gender behaviour. Older siblings, then come into the scene as they unconsciously play their part in role imitation. Play socialisation then turns to role learning when gender segregation is apparent as older men teach young boys in performing their duties and women take the growing girl child under their supervision. In all these processes, the advisory roles of the parents, aunts and uncles and the teachings of grandparents go side by side, internalising gender appropriate behaviour and expectations of the society. Among all these people as agents of socialisation, the role of the mother is continuous right from birth till they attain 18 years, the age limit taken for the present study.

The vista of socialisation within the family, thus, reveals that it is the most significant repository for gender socialisation of the child. It is the epicenter where each member of the family plays their own role in shaping the minds of children to gender appropriate values. Has there been any change in the role of family as an agent of socialisation or does it still stands as it were?

Investigation on the perspective of change on family as an agent of socialisation shows that similar functions and responsibility were partly held by *longshim* in the past. Young boys and girls spent their evening and night in their respective dormitories. The teachings of elders in the dormitories are inclusive of values and behaviour appropriate to their own gender. The host of the dormitory acted as the disciplinarian and guardian of the inmates. The wards were monitored to perform what is socially sanctioned and shun deviation from what is expected of them in order to maintain social uniformity. For instance, girls were not allowed to go out after sunset while boys were permitted to go for *meisum*. Thus, the dormitory took responsibility for the inmates which in the present context is now wholly performed by individual family with the cessation of dormitory institution.

Family, as an agent of socialisation, plays it part in reproducing gender values from one generation to the other. The value that stands tall on the family pedestal is their patriarchal practices. The authority of the father, for one, is the authentic portrayal of that continuity. This holds true retrospectively with the role the *shimva or shim akhava* (head of the host family) who was the authoritarian head of the dormitory (*Longshim*) of the past. The tradition of this value is apparent till today with the authority of decision-making vested in him as the head of the family. The power relations of women and men thus underlines a strong note of patriarchy where men have authority over their women. The symbolic attributes of such continuity are apparent in the way each member as an agent socialises a girl child and a boy child.

The strand of continuity is also encapsulated in upholding the patrilineal values of the society. Most visible clue is preference given to boys on the basis of their status as the upholder of the family tradition. For instance, the tradition of *naoyan* which gives due importance to a male child as discussed in the previous chapter or the customary tradition of inheritance where women are not entitled to the immovable property and so on, are all significant indicator of continuity indorse by family as an agent of socialisation.

In perpetuating the values of patriliny, a strand of deviation, is however observed in the present times though the adherence to the tradition rooted order of patriliny is still pervasive as a core value. That factor of divergence eclipsing the tradition is the intersection of gender and economy which is introduced with the modern economic set up and education system.

In the past, when the Tangkhuls were largely dependent on their subsistent economy, there was no interference of economic status of a family on gender under any circumstances. Parents and *Longshim* (dormitory), as the agents of socialisation nurture the children into their profession based on gender in separate platform. Economic activities and skills of men and women were streamlined in teaching and in performance irrespective of their economic conditions.

Economy, in the present economic system, is multifaceted. There are units of economy other than the traditional agro-based economic unit where each individual competes in a platform irrespective of their gender. The intersection of gender and economy becomes apparent in such aspect where family as an agent reinforces gender values based on patriliny. The antecedent is based on the data of the three income groups presented in the previous chapter. Boys of low income group and some sections of moderate income group with big number of children, for instance, are favoured over daughters when it becomes a matter of choice. In contrary to this, the economy does not intersect with gender among the high income group and some sections of the moderate income groups of small families with enough resources where the question of choice does not arise. This kind of value which has differential bearings within the same society was not observed in the past. This is, therefore, one aspect of change in which a family as an agent endorses patriliny in socialising a child.

2. Socialisation outside the family

The shapes and patterns of gender are also tailored by the society beyond the family environment. Most children, by the age of four, begin to socialise outside the family. Clues that children do not stay home at this age can be perceived through a common practice of the Tangkhuls; a practice of calling a person on top of the voice and communicating with a person at far distance. A resident of a locality would communicate with another person from another locality by shouting loudly and speaking slowly to enhance audibility. The practice has lost its relevance today with the introduction of mobile telephone. However, the strands of such practice still persist in the way the parents call out to their children at the top of their voice, when they are out playing in the neighbourhood. The practice mentioned here is to stress that children by the age of five, venture beyond their courtyard to play with friends.

In the process of growing up as a girl or a boy, a person goes through different life experiences beyond the home environment in order to conform to the established gendered social norms. There are different factors that act as agents in the process.

(i) Educational Institutions: In the pre–Christianity period, the continuity of the cultural heritage was assured through the indigenous oral traditions. Gender values were internalised in the same way. *Longshim* (dormitories) functions as the educational institution for imparting these traditional values. Internalisation takes place in a separate milieu for the sexes as there were separate dormitories for boys and girls. In Somdal village, there were six *Longshim* – three for girls and three for boys in different localities.

The boys were admitted to the dormitories as soon as they reach puberty. For which the eligible age is normally by 12 or 13. However, before they were taken in to the *Longshim* as eligible members, they were given a probationary period after the performance of a ceremony of distributing a piece of meat called '*sashitsa*'. During this period, they were assigned pre-entry duties and responsibilities of collecting firewood for the dormitory everyday for about three months. The logic in this is to instill discipline and diligence to the boys. Young boys, whose works were found to be satisfactory, were then invited for the dormitory festival known as "*longra phanit*". To mark their entrance as bonafide members of the dormitory, a piece of meat known as "*matemsa*" was distributed to the boys on the day of the festival. For girls, however, no such formalities were observed. They joined the dormitory at a much younger age and leave after marriage.

Longshim acts as a training centre. Different kinds of works were imparted to the wards by elder members of the dormitory. Boys learnt the skills of using spears, spade, axes and handicrafts like bamboo-craft, woodcraft, and stone craft. On the other hand, women were taught to spin yarn, weave clothes, stitching, etc. Besides, the oral traditions such as folktales, songs and dances were passed down to the younger generations in the institution. This way, they learn duties expected of a person as a girl or a boy.

Norms and values of each gender were internalised within the group of the dormitory. The credence of the ideals of femininity and masculinity were reinforced by the *Longshim* in more ways than one. The values of soft-spoken personality, for instance, were taught to the girls as from time to time they entertain visitors in the dormitory. They were taught to remain inside the dormitory after sunset. This was imposed to maintain the standards of morality expected of her as a woman. In the same way, men were taught to shoulder his authority with dignity and uphold the ideal values appropriate to a patriarch. Men, for instance, were taught to be courageous, decisive, and daring which portray the standards set by the culture as ideal for a man. Thus, dormitories functioned as agents of socialisation in strengthening its value system.

The institution was a platform for the members to exhibit their excellence in learning. Competitions were held among members of the same gender to prove their skills acquired in the institution. The festivals were also commonly held for the dormitories as well as for the youths to exhibit the talents and skills. The skill of women in weaving, for instance, was put to a test during dormitory festival known as *longra phanit*. Clothes woven by women were hung as men throw a bamboo spear through the shawl. If the spear could break through the shawl, then it is disqualified from the set standard but the ones that could repel the spears were considered excellent. Likewise, men were dared to wrestle with the fellow men to test their strength. Their competence in their agricultural activities was also put to test. Hunting trips were also organised for men to prove their prowess. Those persons with excellent skills were known as *khamarapva* (girl) *or khamarapa* (boys).

In this traditional institution, the values appropriate to each gender were tutored by senior members. Education for boys was concentrated on subjects touching political, social, economic and cultural values, while that of the girls' dormitory dealt with social, cultural and economic values. Values imparted through this institution came in different shades as dormitories accommodated only members of the same sex.

The dormitory system continued for some years even after the advent of Christianity. The new faith and the introduction of modern education eclipsed this age-old institution as it replicated to some other forms. Continuity of dormitory institution as an agent of socialisation was traced to locate its replication. The nearest to the said institution is the modern education system with its functions similar to that of the old traditional setup. To elicit a lucid picture of the transition from one to the other, a look at the brief history of how the people responded to the shift will unravel the vistas of the socio-cultural context.

The introduction of formal education in Ukhrul could be traced to the arrival of the first American missionary in 1896. A primary school was set up in the same year with enrolment of 30 students. The response of people was very negligible until the then superintendent Major Maxwell ordered the village chiefs to send their children to school. He also warned them strictly on attendance to which the children complied, not with the zeal to learn, but out of fear.

The first school in the area, Phadang LP School was set up in 1905 at Phadang village adjacent to the field of the present study. The first batch of students (20 boys) from the village was enrolled that year. The village elders selected the boys from the village every year to attend school till a temporary building was set up in the village by the local missionary in 1919. Only boys selected from different clans were enrolled in the initial years while girls substituted the duties of boys in the economic activities. Gradually, the schools expanded and at present the village has three schools – a government funded Somdal Ningkhalem High School, a community run Ruichumhao Memorial School and an Autonomous District Council funded Kasom Lower Primary School attended by all children irrespective of gender.

Education in the village has today occupied an important place in their culture. It is now a means to meet emerging economic imperatives. This changing perspective towards education is the reason why even illiterate parents want to ensure that their children get education to enjoy better life. Education, according to their concept, is correlated with status in the society. This accentuates on a new hierarchy which establishes a social order based on educational status. However, the question of going beyond gender and individualising a person with the status is posited with an ambiguity as the status itself is foreground with patrilineal values of their culture.

The burgeoning changes in every aspect of the Tangkhuls with the introduction of modern education are apparent as it unwinds its course through the entire gamut of their culture. *Longshim* discontinued but minute analysis was taken up to examine if the traditional learning centre could be located in a replicated form as agent of socialisation in the present context. Based on the function as agent of socialisation, schools partly take on the role of *Longshim.*

Situating the present educational institution vis-à-vis the traditional institution of *Longshim*, the most apparent change is the structure of the institution which can be discussed from the perspective of enrolment. The traditional institutions were set up separately for each sex with different set of gender values. The continuity of this structure was visible for a while in the present educational institution as girls were not allowed to attend school. However, girls too were inducted into schools.

There have been changes along the way as *longshim* replicates to Schools if we analyze this from the perspective of socialisation. One aspect of change is membership to these institutions. It was mandatory for all children of the village to get enrolled in the *Longshim*. And that any member of the *Longshim* was not allowed to stay at home without attending the dormitory except for ill health. The educational institution in the present day, however, is a matter of choice based on economic factor and parental preference.

Modern educational institution, as an agent of socialisation takes us to another spectrum of change where it facilitates wider space for the child's socialisation. Unlike the days of dormitory where socialisation was confined within children of a village, they are today exposed to wider arena. Children of the upper age group today move out after their 10th standard to pursue further studies. Thus, they are exposed to other cultural values with which they did not grow up with. If we place women under the measurement of change in this aspect, it can be mentioned here that women were not allowed to venture outside the village for security reason in the past. There were instances of boys paying visits to the girl's dormitory to and from the neighbouring villages but this kind of liberty was never allowed to women.

Changes in modern formal education system vis-à-vis the *Longshim* could also be read in creating platform for the wards, which is very significant against the background of gender analysis. The old educational institution streamlined separate platform for the sexes and internalisation of gender values took place within the segregated institution as per the demarcated gender values sanctioned by the society. In contrary to old system, the modern formal education systems submerge the differences as it presents a common platform for competition. The reverberation of this could be read in the deviation of the orthodox societal norm of debarring women from public platform. For instance, in the pre–Christian era, it was not permissible for women to make any public address. In the present context, however, such androcentric hegemony could no longer exhibit its vivacity in some aspects of their lives like educational institutions and to some extent in the religious institution. But it does not surmount to deny the fact that continuity of such rigid patriarchal fabric forms the core in the traditional social and political institutions.

There is not even a single aspect of educational institution as an agent that withstand change as discussed and not all things have lost its values as it continues through is a replication in some way or the other. The purpose of attending such institutions remains more or less the same in the former and the latter as the objective is a quest for life skills. For the members of the dormitory, it was mandatory to learn everything taught in the dormitories. In similar manner, students learn according to the curriculum formulated by schools. The differentiation sets in when it is analyzed from the perspective of gender. The curriculum of girls dormitory, for instance, was limited only to the feminine values and women oriented skills whereas in the present educational institution, choice of disciplines is largely optional without gendered curriculum streamlining. This unfolds a new outlook which goes beyond the traditional norms. Interaction with some children who sketched out their outlook of life and the reality conditioned by the social standard as recorded are given hereunder.

Case 22: *For a 13-year old girl, Asing, the primary purpose of attending school is to pursue science after graduating from high school. She aims to become a doctor. The young girl is inspired by a woman in her village, who works as a doctor in the state capital.*

In many occasions, the girl had seen the lady attending to the sick in the village whenever she came home for Christmas. On the part of her parents, the purpose of sending her to school is simply to place her in a white-collared job and make her economically independent in future. But at the same time, the parents are uncertain of her future education. There is a lingering question whether they will be able to support her for further studies as she has four other siblings.

Case 23: *Angam, a father of three children, is very happy for his daughter who is due to complete her engineering studies. In the first place, he simply sent her to college to get a graduate degree. He never expected her to go that far in her pursuit for education. He was against his daughter's idea of pursuing engineering, considering his limited income. After much persuasion, he however relented to his daughter's request. Today, he is a proud father.*

Case 24: *Athing is a tenth standard student in a local school. For him, the purpose of attending school is to get a university degree and find a stable job. His intention, after completing his studies, is to look out for greener pasture beyond the village. With limited prospect to progress in life, he cannot imagine life in village as a cultivator toiling in the sun and rain.*

A close examination on the attitude of children and parents indicates how education has changed the perception of the people. The outlook expressed in the above case studies present the package of education, which was not the case in the past. This is accentuated by economic imperatives in which the traditional economy could no longer sustain them with the increasing population and the changing lifestyle. Therefore, most parents, with every possible means, invest on education of their children.

Continuity of the old education system, however, cannot be rout out as they are apparent in certain aspects of education related values. Honor accorded to a learned individual is, for one, a common value associated with the traditional as well as the modern education. Thus, this factor is apparently a trace of continuity. In the past, persons who were conversant with customary laws or have prowess in physical combat or skilled in any other economic activities were highly admired and respected. This traditional ideal has now taken the form of educational qualification.

The focal point of discussion here on continuity is also apparent in the way they endorse the value of patriliny in education which is revealed through the intersection of economy and gender, as discussed in the family, where girls of the lower income group are debarred from higher education when the resources are limited.

Taking all these accounts into consideration, it can be said that the changes in this institution is one of the most powerful influence which brought about changes in gender socialisation of children.

(ii) Religion: Gender is deeply embedded in the structure of religion. Among the Tangkhuls, the traditional religion at the village level is a complete portrayal of their patriarchy where women were not allowed to hold any office or address public meeting. In this regard, they were equated with children. Women and children were not even allowed to enter sacrificial places and participate in rituals and ceremonies pertaining to the community. It was only attended by adult men where the village chief holds the highest post assisted by the *sharwo* (priest), known as *shimthui luithui khamiya* (specifically in this village) and the *hangva* (clan representatives or clan heads).

The extension of religious duties of the Tangkhuls to the family level is observed in the traditional religion. The head of the family acts as the *sharwo* (priest) assisted by his wife, who could be considered as the priestess of the family which however is restrained within the domestic domain. The role of women is visible in family rite like *shimshar* (household genna). In this context, family functioned as an independent sub-unit of their community religion. In certain occasions like *shimshar* (household genna), or in rituals like warding off evil spirits, women performed the rituals together with their husbands.

Chumphu phanit, a festival marking the opening of their granary after the year's harvest. The role of women in rituals was significant in this festival as she performs the necessary ritual while prohibition was imposed on men from sleeping in the house on the eve before the ritual. The prohibition is also extended to their tools and weapons which should not be kept indoors. The next day, as a ritualistic practice, men had to go for fishing and hunting.

Women's pivotal role in religious activities is visible during this festival as they performed rituals of offering prayer to the *ameowa* (Supreme Being) before taking out paddy from the granary. The significance of this ritual is to seek blessing upon the stock of the granary to last the entire year. On the day of the ritual, however, women were to take the stock for the day itself. This ritual is also associated with avoidance of the opposite sex in which women tried to be as discreet as possible not to meet men on their way to collect the paddy from the granary, as this was considered a bad omen during the period. Traditionally, the spatial location of the granary in the Tangkhul villages is constructed a little farther away from the dwelling house. The same evening, dinner is prepared with rice from the newly harvested paddy complemented with items like meat or fish brought by men of the family from the day's expedition.

The festivity ends with a ceremony known as *zavar.* Women take out paddy from the granary and dry the paddy in the sun and pound them. While drying the paddy, they had to make sure that fowl and birds do not pick up a single grain as it was considered a bad omen. This ceremony was followed by *veishir*, closing of the village gate where men replace the old gate with a new one. This was done to secure the village from any enemy's threat.

To situate the role of women against the cultural context of the Tangkhuls, it needs to demonstrate the indispensable role of women in sustaining the economy. The role of women in rituals of the household embodies the fundamental connection between women and economic management of the household. Thus, women's role in the rituals of the family is relative to the degree of their role in the economy as they tow the line of the economic front as the *akhavaiva* (lady of the house). The pivotal role of women in religious rituals is however confined within the domain of the family. They are debarred to perform rituals at the community level among the Tangkhuls. But the fact is that women were never a priestess of the community. Her role as a priestess never did cross beyond the family domain.

The traditional religion, as an agent of socialisation conditions women and men with hegemonic sanctions of what should and should not be performed by each gender. The norms and values of religion had a strong grip in the minds of the people and actions which were manifested in the adherence to the traditional rooted superstitions and ingrained religious sanctions of what a woman or man can do or cannot do. Women and men learnt to stay in their demarcated patriarchal order for fear of the supernatural forces. They perform their respective duties expected of them as women or men. This way, the gendered religious values were passed down from generation to generation.

The advent of Christianity saw the eclipse of the traditional religion with the arrival of the first missionary Reverend William Pettigrew in 1895. It marked the beginning of mission work among the Tangkhuls. But it was only in 1901 that the first batch of 12 converts was made out of his students. Tracing the history of Somdal, the advent of Christianity first took place when a local Rs. Ruichumhao first started the missionary work in the village. In the early years of Christianity, restrictions were not strictly imposed on the converts. They were allowed to drink rice beers and follow some traditional practices fearing total elimination might lead to severe opposition from the local people as the doctrine was alien to the Tangkhuls. Gradually, more and more people started their conversion and the traditional practices were totally abandoned by 1923.

In the early years of Christianity, there was no regular worship place in the village. The converts gathered at different places alternately. The construction of the Church building started in January, 1923 and was dedicated on the 7th of May the same year.

In the present institution of the Church, there are certain demarcations on the basis of gender even though men and women take equal participation in all religious ceremonies and in the Church assembly, which is the decision-making body. The main religious body comprises of pastors (only men occupy the chair till date), deacons and deaconess (87% men and 12% women), the choir (50% women and 50% men), the youth wings (chaired by men till date), women wings (which comprises of only married women) and the children department (comprising of all the children of the church members).

The present Church organisation as an agent of socialisation is a continuation of the smaller unit of their traditional religion - the religious unit of family. Despite the changes, continuity can be located in the structure of these institutions. Continuation of the traditional system could be underlined in the structure of these institutions. In the past family priest is none other than the father. In similar way, the head of the present church organisations are men which are represented by the chair of the pastor. The other dignitaries namely the deacons and deaconess, assist the head of the institution as in the past religious unit of family, in which the priest of the family was assisted by his wife in performing the family rituals and ceremonies.

Membership of the institutions is another illustration of continuity. The Church institution and the traditional family as religious unit have representations of other members, which constitute the congregation of the institutions. In the traditional system, other members of the family form this congregation including both genders. Likewise, the present religious unit is represented by members of the church, the congregation of which is formed by different societies like the children department, Christian youth society, women society, choir members, etc.

The structure and function of these institutions show certain changes with the present church organisation having a wider network. The religious unit of the family as an agent of socialisation is limited within the ambit of the family. It functioned independently from the bigger village religion, the structure and function were confined within the family members.

The function of the present Church organisation, unlike the traditional family unit, encompasses all members of the village. It also extends its functions beyond the domain of their local Church. It is affiliated to the bigger organisation of the tribe like the Tangkhul Baptist Churches Association, which is again an affiliated member of the state level organisation, Manipur Baptist Convention and so on. The Church organisation as an agent, thus, provides platform to the children in diversified activities. It organizes Bible camps, youth conferences, district level gatherings and so on and thereby rendering children with exposure beyond the village.

(iii) *Yarnao* (Peer Group): The Tangkhuls use the term '*yarnao*' to designate a peer group, which is based on the age of individuals. The formation of such groups starts by the age of six. In the past such groups manifest their solidarity through work and festivities. Social festivities of such groups show equal participation of both boys and girls. Such festivities were known as *yarra phanit*. Celebration of youth is the theme of such festival with feasting, competitions and exhibition of skills and merry making are important features of the festival.

The *yarra* festival commonly falls in the month of April. Festivities were taken up only in the morning, evening and at night. During the day they go about with their respective works. They made preparations of food before the festival and the best beer was given to the village chief and the clan heads on the eve of the festival. This was done as a form of taking permission and acknowledgement of such festivities. The celebration went on even for a month.

The basis of peer formation in the present context is not solely based on age as in the past. This may be held responsible to different factors knitted together with change that has taken place in the society. The degeneration of the old dormitory system is partly responsible for the discontinuation of such traditional criterion of peer groups as it losses relevance with the present social and educational set up. The lack of cohesion of the old concept is accentuated by the cessation of *yarra* festivities which was discontinued simultaneously with the dormitory system. To evaluate the determinants of peer groups, the factors for the formation of peers were examined in the following cases.

Case 25: *For the youths in the village, Christmas is a time they look forward to with anticipation. Beside the religious fervor, it is a time for reunion as most youths, in the present context, do not stay home for* *further studies or due to their profession. The reunion of friends would be associated with gathering, especially bonfire at night and dinner party. Their get together would often go till midnight as they sing and chat by the bonfire. When I was in a village, I noticed a group of youths who caught up together after 15 years. My curiosity led me to investigate on how they formed the group years ago.*

A member of the group, ***Aphy****, who is a 30-year-old woman, narrated to me how they formed this peer group (yarnao) when she was in the ninth standard at school***.*** *The group was formed within a circle of school friends who helped each other in school activities. From then on, they extended their association to other activities like organising rotational labour exchange (yarthot) for agricultural works during their holidays. The group comprises five boys and seven girls.*

All of them went about their own way to pursue higher studies and career after high school. Their frequent visits and group activities in the village were punctuated owing to relocation of most members to different places.

The bond of friendship shared by the group of friends is an illustration of how people in the village environment form their peer groups and how they maintain that solidarity later on in life. This way, peer group is formed out of different circumstances.

Case 26: *The tradition of meisum (fireside gathering) is a practice which every youth looked up to whenever they are free from their duties. This practice may sound so strange to some but to put it in simple words, it is a way of relaxing and entertainment as youths gather over a cup of tea and ethnic snacks like pancakes made out of sticky rice flour. This practice happens to be one factor of structuring peer group.*

Thotyar, *a group of teenagers, is formed out of their association through meisum. A group of boys initially formed this group, the membership for which was also later extended to girls. The group consists of 36 members. The name '****thotyar****,' literally means peer or friends of a same generation.*

The objective of forming the group is multifarious. They organise labour exchange programme among the members, and also works for the welfare of the village community through various social service programmes. They have also taken up cleaning drive, tree plantation and extend help through labour assistance too. The group generates funds through various means and some funds are kept aside for reunion gatherings.

The age-old tradition of fireside gathering is still very much in practice among the youths. In the past, they gathered at the girls' dormitory which is now replaced by gathering at a girl's residence. The case mentioned is an illustration that this tradition provides platform to form peer groups and acts as agents of socialisation.

***Case** 27: A group of children playing together in the courtyard or running around in group is a common sight in a village. The most common form of peer formation develops within the circle of neighbourhood children, though factors of peer formation are varied as they frequently come together to play.*

A group of eleven girls were busy playing counting games in a big courtyard. It is played by forming two teams; one team would throw a handmade ball (made out of unused loose socks) targeting a slap of wooden plank turn by turn among a team. On hitting the slap, they would try to stamp on the slap and make counts to reach certain numbers while they try to protect their body from the swirling throws with their hands from hitting their body. On the other hand, the other team throws the ball to the counting team trying to hit their body.

The group formed a perfect picture of a girl's peer group. This group is formed among the circle of childhood friends in a particular locality though the houses are not within a stone-throw distance. The members of the group are not of the same age. Every bustle, outside the social or school activities and household chores, are performed within the circle of this group. Their playtime would often be Sunday afternoons. A festival is another fun time for the members of the group as they would dine together with merrymaking. The seasonal breaks from school are another moment for the group to get together as they would perform agricultural duties in group in rotational basis.

The case studies present different factors responsible for peer group formation. It helps to underline, how in the village set up, circumstances shape peer groups among one's gender or between boys and girls. The first case represents how peers of childhood days, pervades beyond the stage and maintains the group solidarity at adult stage. The second case represents how socialisation at the adolescent period through *meisum* encourages group solidarity culminating to formation of peers group. The third case represents the most common factor of peer groups among children of the neighbourhood. These cases also present the role of the peers through their activities at various stages.

Delving into the concept of *yarnao* and what it embodies in the context of the society, another structure of such group is found in the religious institution. The grading system could be located in the youth wings under the umbrella of Church organisation. The classification of the grades is tabled as follows:

Table 14: Grades of the Christian Youth Society

Grade	Criteria
Learning Society	Right after baptism but who have not entered youth society
Junior Society	Those who have been newly inducted into the youth society
Intermediate Society	Upgrade into this group as they mature and as younger members join the junior group
Senior Society	Men continue to be member even after they get married; women on the other hand, remain in the group till they get married.

Source: Fieldwork.

All members of the first grade (learning society) and some members of the second grade (junior society) fall within the age group of the present study. As such these grades were taken as parameters to study the peer groups.

The first and foremost principle of the grade system which tantamount it to the concept of the traditional *yarnao* (peer) is the grades based on age which may however vary slightly as the present grades incorporate certain age cohort within each grade. Secondly, it maintains group solidarity among its members. It thus serves as a repository of the traditional peer group of the past which can be traced as continuity.

The norm that sums the grades of the youth society as an agent of gender socialisation can be situated in the functions of the grades which outline dichotomised values in itself. The main purpose is to assist in the activities of the Church organisation. The activities of these groups include performance of duties and activities grade-wise for the welfare of the Church and based on the religious values of the religious institution. For instance, these groups take turns in cleaning the Church and assist in every manual works of the institution which is based on gendered division of labour.

The activities of the group could also be located through grade-wise participation in Church programmes or participation in song competitions during the festivals. The group participation in such activities, at face value, paints a portrait of an egalitarian relations which is rather deceptive. Hidden under such heap of mass participation is riddled with contradictions where lies the inner reality of hegemony defined androcentric norms. The reason is not far to seek as the group and organisation functions under the leadership of men. The activities of these groups though confined within the religious domain pervades over other spheres of their lives. The status quo maintained in the process of socialisation within this groups help shape the mindset in conforming to the norms of gender values uphold by the society.

The structure and nature of peer group, as discussed, have witnessed certain changes augmented by the vicissitudes of their lifestyle. The structure which orders changes in the characteristics of peer groups is enhanced by the elements of modernity which put an end to the conservative village centered worldview. As can be pictured through the description of the past, traditional *yarnao* was confined within the circle of the village. *Yarnao* which emerged out of their association in the dormitories have been replaced by peers of schools, colleges, professions or through religious grade as mentioned above. Today, the formation of *yarnao* has no border.

Through the years, the tradition-rooted patriarchal values, however, shows perpetuity in the social fabric of the Tangkhul culture. The ingrained social sanction of gender values makes its way through the changing structure. The traditional ideals of femininity and masculinity condition the attitude of the people in shaping patterns of cultural tradition through socialisation.

(iv) Media: Children in the village, as could be deciphered from the way they put up their discussion, talk about looks and dresses they like about celebrities. A boy of nine years was giving a detailed descriptive contour of the hairstyle of a Korean actor which he thinks was perfect and manly. A girl of the same age admiringly looked at a college girl and told her friends that she looks like a Manipuri actress whom she thinks is the embodiment of femininity.

There is no doubt about the influence of media if one goes by the comments of the kids who in their formative mindset formulate the picture of gender through media. The question of how the concept they get through media conditions them to accept and act upon it or how much that concept is in uniformity with the intransigent values of their own is another premise that need thorough investigation. The observation made on children necessitates investigation on media as an agent of socialisation and analysis on changes and continuity.

Media is totally a new agent of socialisation which gives access to knowledge on the imperatives of gender values besides their own. The most popular media in the Tangkhul villages is radio. This is followed by other forms of media like newspapers, television, magazines and internet. However, the village has a limited access to newspaper and magazines due to poor transport and communication supplemented by ignorance by most villagers. The most recent introduction of media is the cellular phone connectivity which has boost internet usage. Of late, there are also televisions with satellite assisted services, but its utility is limited due to irregularity in power supply.

Outlining the role of media in the past, the only channel of communication with the outside world was through village men, who used to travel outside for *lei* (barter trade) and *khayao* (labour trip). It can be recalled here that there was no free access even between the villages keeping aside their contact with the outside world. Even the barter system between villagers was held at the outskirts of the village. As per the data, neighbouring villages of Somdal namely Talui, Ngainga, Phadang, Tuinem and Khampha used to organise fair with the villagers from the north at a particular place called *'paosaitru'*, particularly for barter trade. The spot is located on a small hilltop which forms the border between villages of the north and the western side of the district. The villages of the *raphei* (north) used to bring bamboo products like *sop* (carrying basket), *luk* (storage basket), *kashai* (carrying rope), etc., whereas the *kharaos* (people of the west) used to barter them with their weaving products like *kachon* (shawl) and *kashan* (lower wrap-around garment). Likewise, food grains were also exchanged through these barter systems. This trading system was however carried out only by men and within the tribesmen.

Moving a little further beyond the tribe is their contact with the Meitei, a neighbouring people of the plains. The connection was through labour trip of the Tangkhuls known as *khayao.* The word '*kha*' means village and the '*yao*' means visit. It literally means visiting villages for wage labour. This kind of trip was undertaken during the off-season from their agricultural activities, mostly between February and April with a purpose to earn money by selling their labour. Though the exact period of introduction could not be ascertained, the data indicates that it dated back probably to the emergence of money economy. According to the account given by the key informants, they were paid in terms of coins for their wage. Boys who had already attained the strength of a youth followed the elders during this trip. Women were not allowed to go for this trip for security point of view. With the money they earned, they purchased salt, clothes, and other commodities which were not available in the village.

The means of communication beyond the village in the past could be located in the inconsequential role of *lei* and *khayao.* On analyzing the role of communication of the past, it is clear that women had no direct access to the outside world and thus acquired knowledge and information from men in the village. The traditional communication could not however tantamount to the role of media in gender socialisation as the latter is surmount to a direct agent while the latter is an indirect agent. Change in media as an agent of gender socialisation could be located in the structure and forms of media; the traditional being indirect and one-sided while media today directly influence both genders alike.

Taken together all the agents of gender socialisation, it is clear that gender values are internalised through different channels. The agents get replicated to another structure in course of time. In the present context, continuity of the present agents was traced to the role of the traditional agents which play similar roles in gender socialisation to which it may be concluded that the same institution may not hold the same position when it comes to gender socialisation. For instance, the role and structure of the past family unit is partly taken over by the Church. Likewise, the Church institution need not necessarily be a continuation of the traditional family as religious unit in other cases. The new agent is the old agent in its new array in this context by determining the role of the past and present agents.

It is also apparent that there have been changes in gender relations due to the varied roles of these agents. For instance, *Longshim* as an educational centre imparts different gender values at separate dormitories to boys and girls which are now replaced by schools where education is being imparted on the same platform. Within the school institution, knowledge is imparted equally to everyone irrespective of gender. Opportunities are now open to all but the interference of patrilineal values confines girls of the poorer section within a restricted yard as boys are favoured over girls when resources are limited. This is even true of the fact that femininity can never be defined superseding the decision of men which is continuity of the traditional patriarchy through these agents.

Chapter - V

Summary and Discussion

The different transitions through which an individual passes during their life, at first sight, seem to be biologically fixed from childhood to adulthood and eventually to death. The stages of the course of human life are social as well as biological in nature. They are influenced by biological differences and material circumstances of people's existence in a given type of society. An exploration on gender is gaining salience across many fields, whether indebted to similar frameworks and theories or not. The study on gender has been approached through variegated ways and gender socialisation is one amongst it.

A descriptive account on the culture of Tangkhuls pertaining to gender socialisation has been presented in the previous chapters. Intimate insights into the whole matrix of gender socialisation have been discussed through the structure of how gender operates and through the happenings of everyday life. Internalisation of gender values were studied from the perspective of how children learn through verbal and non-verbal clues at different stages of childhood. The changing gender values were determined through the structure and the role of individuals in the social institution of family, kinship and marriage, which are important units for gender socialisation. Continuity and change in gender relations were determined through agents of socialisation. The study explores gender at three levels:

(i) A child as individual, who internalise her or his identity, and the role of parents and elders, who imbibe gender values through socialisation process.

(ii) The structure of culture that shapes gender relations in the process of socialisation.

(iii) A structured group as agents, who reinforce gender relations through socialisation process.

An attempt to examine the concept of femininity and masculinity calls for both empirical and cognitive approach. It becomes intricate at times to comprehend the logical corollary of their gender ideal with what they practice and the reality may be misconstrued if not verified. This holds true as in the case of male preferences which, for instance, called for such investigation.

In order to conceptualise gender among the Tangkhuls, the verbal and non-verbal clues were studied against the background of the social and cultural setup. Gender values, deeply entrenched in the cultural practices, is reinforced through socialisation. As such, visualisation of such gendered setup starts even before a child could accurately label themselves as *ngalanao* (girl) or *mayarnao* (boy). The range of clues, on the other hand, is unwind by people surrounding the little world of the baby with the way they system differences in their dress and hairstyle, in the way they speak and handle the baby and formulate visual clues for an infant in the learning process. The thematic text of gender in their cultural context is thus tailored to the forms and fit-ins of a child.

Almost every material possession of a child has the preponderance of gender-oriented emphasis between male or female attribute. Practically, all children in fact possess and play with gendered toys. A wooden tricycle (*thingkari*), wooden or clay animal figurines for boys, and dolls or kitchen set toys (*thangthang*) for girls are instances of such playthings exhibiting gendered attributes. The response to such gender stereotyping is being legitimised by parents and elders, who categorically provide the toys to articulate them into the endorsed societal norms. Gender stereotyping of material possession is supplemented with supervision and monitoring of the children to confirm that they do not to deviate from the norms.

Differences in gender attributes stipulate corresponding impact on expectations to women and men. It is in the practices of everyday life that these expectations are fulfilled and reproduced. The expectations encompass, in its entirety, all norms and values that defines femininity and masculinity in their context. A person is expected to perform duties and responsibilities expected of her or him as a girl or boy and as women or men, and act or think in conformity with the established norms of gender.

The analysis of socialisation on executing the gendered expectation shows patriarchal values as the recurrent theme. Likewise, asymmetry in the process of role performance is exceptional where boys shoulder duties that is more strenuous, while girls are expected to take on duties and responsibilities which require more time and patience.

As a person goes through the vicissitudes of life and takes on various fundamental roles, as son or daughter, as mother or father and as grandmother or grandfather, gender socialisation takes on new perspectives though the persistent theme is based on the core value of patriarchy. Learning gender values thus, differs at different stages of a person's life. A perceptible expression can be taken from the change of status of a man from a son to a husband or father who become a *shimva* (householder) and attains membership in his *shangnao* (clan). A woman, on the other hand, changes her status from a *naongalava* (daughter) to an *apareiva* (wife) or *ava* (mother), and establishes a permanent status in her husband's *shangnao*. The role learning thus differs in the status as a boy who learns to be a man to that of a father, who assumes the role as the head of the family.

Socialisation process results in a degree of uniformity among the members of a society as they come to share values and attributes. In order to ensure conformity to the norms of gender values, they are guided by the customary laws with the elders as the guardian of such laws. Parents and elders give guidance to the children as they teach the rules of *ngala khangakhot* (marriage), and *shokhala and vakhalat* (incest). This way, an adolescent child is monitored by elders to stay away from intimate relations with someone from the same clan or unmarriageable cousins as the relationship can lead to incestuous act, whose monitoring is guided by the customary laws.

In the process of relegating the traditional practices, a dichotomy is observed in the way of implementing the rules among boys and girls. For instance, a girl is not allowed to leave the house after dark while permitting boys to go for *meisum* (fireside gathering). This is one typical form of patriarchy, which believes in the principle of men as the initiator in courtship or relationship. According to their customary practices, it is considered a deviation of norms for girls to go after boys. It is always the initiative of boys to start a relationship. This process conditions a boy and a girl into two categories that function together in a culture.

The process of socialisation is bilateral; it is an interaction of what they internalise and what they are fed that includes verbal and non-verbal clues. The structure and structured groups come with pre-conditioned ideals which reinforce itself through stereotyped values. Manifestation underpinning such stereotyping is palpable in the way parents and elders tailor gendered material things to young children. Thus, children absorb the stereotyped values, which supplement the internalising process of locating where they ought to be.

The construction of femininity and masculinity through the prism of socialisation shows hegemony with patriarchy as the core value. It is woven into the social fabric where signifier is expressed in social terms like *akhava* (head), *shang akhava* (clan head), *Awunga* (village chief), and *shimluikat* (upholder of the family's tradition), etc. All these terms describe men as the head of their social institution. Juxtaposing these terms with the terminologies they use for women like *shim akhavaiva* (wife of the head of family) or *shang akhavaiva* (wife of the clan's head), it is clear that the identity of women is subsumed with that of their men. These terms are also associated with their power as owner of her husband's property, whose rights however does not tantamount to ownership of it as an individual.

Manifestation of patrilineal values is apparent in the attitude of gender favouritism. A representation of such expression is tangible in rituals such as *naoyan* and *naoming kaphok*, where importance given to a boy child is associated with the ritual discussed earlier. In case of the birth of a female child, these rituals do not hold the credence as that of a male child or may also be given amiss. *Naoyan*, which literally means 'baby seeing' is a symbolical declaration of the new arrival in the family. The figurative connotation thus, underlines the importance of a male child as the upholder of the family tradition. In the same way, *naoming kaphok* (naming ceremony) of a daughter does not come with feasting and merrymaking. Such celebrations are endowed only to sons.

The ideological exploration on the attributes of femininity and masculinity projects contrasting gender ideals. In the background of the traditional ideals with men as the protector of their women and children, and the practices of men at warfare, the boys are ingrained to be rough and daring; the ideal which still is an appendage with the values of masculinity. Men may not literally go to war today, but the relevance of this value still fetters men to stand for their women and children when their rights are being infringed. When they perform this kind of duties, they are expected to do it courageously with their head held high. The symbolic expression projects men to be more aggressive than women. The standard of expectation thus places men as the protector, which connotes superiority over the ones being protected. Women, on the other hand, co-operates with it in their own subordination.

Femininity in its all-pervading metaphor is authentically depicted in the girl's role imitation during their play session. The entire gamut of women's role as a sister, as a wife and a mother in real life is portrayed when small girls take on the role of their adults. Women oriented values, termed as *ngalakashok* (feminine) encompass values like caring (*sheba sakathei)*, understanding (*phapkata)*, and *takui kahai* (tenderness) all paint the picture of feminine ideals. The esteem that a woman enjoys as a woman is relative to the degree that she settles into these roles or values. One cannot circumvent and overlook the fact that these values are indicative of the home-centric nature of woman. This emanates from the gendered division of labour where women occupy the domestic front. Small girls sweet-talking with their toys and busy playing kitchen divulge the nurturing and domestic sides of women which are an appendage to femininity.

Juxtaposing the identity of the sexes as women and men within a broad social context of the Tangkhuls, the female identity is aligned to that of men. A woman's status as a daughter or wife is classified with that of men - as daughter of her father and as wife of her husband. A daughter is never identified officially with her mother's clan. This holds the same credence even in cases of divorced parents and illegitimate cases as children are affiliated to the father's clan. A woman after marriage is naturally affiliated to her husband's family. Thus, a woman's identity is subsumed with their men which are symbolical representation of their patriliny.

One cannot circumvent or overlook the fusion of the traditional and the cultural imperatives of the outside world which, in other words can be termed as modernity. The substantiation is lucid with generational comparative analysis. Gender roles, for instance, elicit a fresh look in the process of investigation as the gap is perceptible in the way elderly people view younger generations with critical candour on how they perform gendered duties and responsibilities. A wife in a traditional society was all but a wife and the epicenter of her universe was home and family within the boundary of their village. The home-centric nature emanated from the situation of those times where women's movement beyond the village was not advisable due to inter-village feuds and that participation in the public sphere was minimal with exception of participation in festivities. The situation thus left gender roles of women in a marginalised position.

The current scene shows a different picture which necessitates a comprehensive recognition of women outside the domestic sphere too, without overlooking her roles at the home front. Today, a woman spread her wings beyond the domestic boundary as she shares financial responsibility with their man as breadwinner. The present situation therefore demands changes in gender roles which becomes the path breaker on the traditional setup. Thus, gender is not a fixed characteristic. It comes out in context of a particular encounter. Gender, as such, change with time and reproduces itself through gender socialisation. What was considered as something that is totally masculine may be shared by today's women and vice versa.

Eclipse of the old tradition as response to the imperatives of changing times has impacted gender socialisation in more ways than one. The legitimised responsibility that comes with patrilineal descent is the obligation of men towards the aged parents and unmarried siblings, and the credence of its responsibility is even bigger for the eldest son with him inheriting the ancestral property and the lion's share. The rigid code of the tradition has lost its vivacity as responsibility of care for the aged parents is shared by all practically, which bears as an example to the growing children who will shoulder the same responsibility later on in his life.

Against the perspectives on how kin groups maintain solidarity among the older generations through the usage of terminologies, exchange of foods, help, goods, visits, etc., the present symbolic expression of kin solidarity was evaluated to unearth elements of how gender attributes wind its course through the years. Its impact on gender values as a whole in its trajectory is significant in the way the intimacy of the kin group being infringed by relocation of people to different places and the rigid code of gendered terminologies which have lost its vigour. Evaluating the changes through the prism of gender socialisation, the picture of divergence from the old tradition is apparent.

One most significant determinant that underscores the evolving gender relations is the issue of dependent and independent existence of each sex. This condition has its corresponding impact on gender roles and at times, raises its head even in the decision-making of the family. The study shows that the currency-based economy shows placement of women in a better position as compared to the past trend, particularly in their say when it comes to financial decision-making in the family and this obviously sets an example to the children. Could it really bridge gender disparity in power relations? This is a question which needs an in-depth analysis.

Education is perceived as the means to financial independence. Enrolment of children in schools is the tangible evidence as every children of the village are enrolled. The façade of school enrolment seems to premise gender equity at a glance. The overt picture, however, cannot be lulled into complacency as it is riddled with contradictions and complexities. As discussed, the interference of patrilineal values finds its symbolic expression in the intersection of economy and gender, where the exigency of economy always comes with gender preference. The simple logic could be deducted in the way parents favour boys with better schools and higher education in times when their financial constraint pushes them to a matter of choice. Thus, the picture hidden under the heap of all children of a family being enrolled in schools is tainted with gender preference in reality.

The socialisation process though traditional is exposed to many external forces that conspire to the tradition rooted conventions and have undergone many twists and turns. An exposure of people to the outside world and the forces of modernity can be dated back to the advent of Christianity amongst the Tangkhuls. The village under study had celebrated their Church centenary in the year 2009. The changes brought about by Christianity are augmented by the introduction of modern education system that has changed their world view and their way of life. The outlook of people further saw transformation with better transport and communication paving ways for inflow and outflow of their culture. Intermarriage is one tangible expression of change in their social institution which witnessed an extension of their kinship ties far and wide, and also a route for exchange of values.

The coalescence of traditional and modern elements of culture is patent. The influx of external elements is apparent in the outlook of the children and the way they adapt to the ways of the outside world. This is however, not to deny the fact that traditional values too co-exist with the modern ways of life. The perpetuity of the traditional values could be seen in the way children dichotomize themselves to the gendered behaviour;

gendered roles and responsibilities, sticking to the stereotyped playthings among other things are rudimentary repositories of the traditional cultural practices. These tangible values represented through the symbolic expression thus, foreground the fact that no amount of modernity could dilute their traditional values altogether. These values coexist, replicate or blend together in the process of socialisation.

The unprecedented changes in their cultural practices relating to gender are a response provoked by modernity. These responses are shaped by new circumstances. The vistas of the changing circumstances can be viewed through the spectrum of economic vicissitude through the years. For multiple reasons, traditional subsistence economy, which was the backbone of their economy, could no longer sustain their livelihood. This, in turn, calls for other supplementary sources of sustenance. The mode of exchange from the traditional barter system to the money economy brought about drastic shift in their economic practices.

The economic transformation takes us to the other end of the spectrum and introduces a new status structure with the redefinition of the concept of wealth. This is the juncture, where the status of each sex intersects as individualisation rise its head minimally minimising the shade of gender to certain extent. Women, who could never exercise their rights in decision-making at the family level now enjoy certain liberty to express their views, though they are not allowed to be assertive. In similar way, a man who is economically dependent on his wife is more likely to consult with his wife in certain aspects of decision-making. Money economy, thus, bridged a petite space of gender disparity in decision-making, which however is limited to financial matters as patriarchy transcends all other values that set the center-stage for gendered practices.

The agents of socialisation play a defining role in bringing about changes as well as in preserving the traditional values. Tracing through these agents, the changes in gender socialisation and continuity of the built-in core values surfaces. The transmission of values through socialisation process by different agents, however, take different forms with new circumstances. Gender socialisation is juxtaposed against the cultural setup of the Tangkhuls, which poignantly conveys that the same agents of gender socialisation do not play the same role in imparting values through these years. The vigilant role of the *shimkhur* (family), for instance, to an adolescent child was shared by *longshim* and the family in the past.

In the process of tracing the roles of socialising agents, the emergence of new agents of socialisation like media or the church organisation is apparent, which is but the replication of roles of some traditional agents of socialisation. In this context, the application is limited to socialisation and may not yield the same result otherwise. The empirical evidence is suggestive of the fact that the structured groups imparting the values have changed triggered by a set of circumstances that shape their lives. The structure of the dormitory system of the past could not survive today as it becomes unsuitable in the modern times. Likewise, the earlier practice of *khayao* becomes irrelevant today with the introduction of other economic avenues.

In the face of the multi-faceted changes that apparently show in their practices, the culture is stringed with rigid patriarchal code which never let their guards down. As such the core values of patriarchy and patriliny are closeted safely in their culture. The way the Tangkhuls organise various institutions, the language they use to describe femininity and masculinity, all point to the fact that gender values of the Tangkhuls are very much intact from external factors. Even the intersection of gender and economy in the present times and the responses of male preference to such circumstances are indicative of their age-old gender values.

According to the findings, it can thus be concluded that gender values have not experienced drastic change. In spite of the continuity of gender values, there is no doubt, that the trends of gender socialisation have changed with changing gender roles. Taking all accounts together, it can be concluded that the predominant cultural circumstances condition gender socialisation of children which cannot tantamount in diluting their core patriarchal or patrilineal values.

Gender socialisation is one perspective of important parameters that determines gender relations. As the study shows, gender relations start right from how an infant take clues of what it is to be a girl or a boy. Amongst the Tangkhuls, it is found that a person's later adult life is always controlled by values that one internalised during childhood. No amount of external forces could dilute the deeply rooted values.

A study on gender as a fundamental category among the Tangkhul tribe, through the lens of gender socialisation, is an attempt to enhance knowledge of cultural studies in the academic analysis. Unlike women studies which focus only on women or the earlier anthropological studies that were criticized for male oriented approach of considering only men's voice as the representation of a culture, the present study analyzes gender on the basis of gender socialisation exploring the connectivity between what it means to be a woman and what it is to be a man. In doing so, it includes the exploration of both differences and similarities between these two categories. Also unlike the approach of feminism that seeks solely from women's perspective, the present study takes the perspective of relations between men and women.

The present research work, I believe, would come in handy to some extent beyond the academic realm, to assess various programmes and activities as it gives the picture of a culture through the lens of gender. In recent time the relevance of gender studies has surpassed the limits of academic interest. It has now emphasised its importance of applying critical gender analysis in all areas of social life and its impact on areas such as law, politics, science, education, art, commerce, psychology and health. By basing on the principles and methods of critical inquiry, gender studies lead to in-depth awareness of social life. It teaches skills in critical thinking, development of one's own understandings and communication of one's ideas. Gender studies enables us to question how gender as a social and cultural construction shape people's lives, their relationships, the workplace, institutional structures, public policy and the production of knowledge.

Thus, gender studies have emerged as an indispensable aspect in the framework of social and economic process. It elicits a fresh understanding to the policy makers in implementing development programmes. In different sectors, social and economic policies are drafted and adopted with particular emphasis on gender, the assessment and evaluation of societal progress of which is based on the mechanism of gender equity. Until recently, its relevance was rather ignored or overlooked, but with time gender study has permeated different levels of social and economic process.

Glossary

Achon : Elder sister
Achon kharar : Eldest sister
Agahara : Husband
Ahanglui : Jhum field
Akhaishang : Thigh
Akhamei : Tail
Akhava : Head
Akhavaiva : Wife of akhava
Akui : Head
Akuisa : Head parts
Amei : Elder brother
Amei kharar : Eldest brother
Ameowa : Supreme being
Amak : Brother-in-law
Amakei : Kidney
Amalung : Heart
Amathin : Liver
Ani : Aunt / mother-in-law
Apā : Sister to younger brothers
Apareiva : Wife
Arangkung : End part of the backbone
Arihava : Daughter-in-law
Ashilat : Gizzard
Athei asa : Relatives (both maternal and paternal)
Avā : Father
Ava : Mother
Avākato : Father's younger brother
Avąkatui : Mother's younger sister
Avākharar : Father's elder brother
Avąkharar : Mother's elder sister

Ava wui naongalava	: Father's daughter
Awo	: Uncle / grandfather / father-in-law
Awo-ayi khararchan	: Folktale
Awunga	: Village chief
Ayi	: Grandmother
Chan khangazek	: Assembly
Chakshang	: Kitchen
Chinaongara	: Siblings
Chipee	: Malevolent spirit
Chonlan	: A practice where shawls and lower garments are given as presents or gifts to the relatives on occasions like marriage, merit feast, funerals, death anniversary, festivals, etc.
Chonsrui	: Eldest sister; usually refers to the wife of village chief.
Chumphu	: Festival marking the beginning of taking out newly harvested grains from the granary.
Dharma	: Religion
Fathuikhalui	: Remarriage on the part of women.
Gahara	: Husband
Hangva.	: Village Authority
Hao kuiret	: Boys shave their hair at the sides leaving a patch of hair from the front till the back of the head which they call Hao kuiret.
Harra Khayang	: Egg Divination
Harkho Khayang	: Cock Divination
Hok	: Pig
Ichichashi	: Literally, it means own group which covers all agnatic relations on the father's side.
Ikato	: My younger brother (men to younger men)
Ikatuiva	: My younger sister (women to younger women)
Imuilava	: My sister-in-law
Izarva	: My younger sister (men to younger women).
Kachon	: Shawl
Kapa Khayang	: Bamboo divination
Kapai	: Jump
Kaphara	: Birth
Kari	: Motor vehicle (Toy vehicle in the context)
Karphang	: Hoe
kashai	: A rope used for carrying basket
Kashan	: Lower garment
Kashong Kahao	: Festival celebrated to protect the crops
Kathi kasar	: Death ceremony
Keithei	: Market

Kha	:	Village
Khainao	:	Knife
Khaipak	:	Dao
Khaita/Mawonzai	:	Festival offering prayers to the god of wealth to protect their crops from hailstorms and other calamities
Khamarapa	:	Skilled man
Khamarapva	:	Skilled woman
Khangayei	:	A term used to refer to a transformed animal form by human being.
Khangkathei	:	Patient
Khanong	:	Traditional medical practitioner
Khararnaosan	:	Senior members
Khayao	:	Naga labour trip
Lairikshim	:	School
Lairik tamkhangarumbing	:	Classmate
Larar	:	Spinster
Longra Phanit	:	Dormitory festivals
Longshim	:	Dormitories
Luira	:	Seed sowing festival
Luk	:	Storage basket
Mahar	:	A tall plant
Malung makazang	:	Coward
Mangkha	:	Festival after the completion of their paddy plantation
Maran kasa	:	Merit feast
Mari kashem	:	Metallurgy
Matemsa	:	Meat distributed to the boys to mark their membership in the dormitory
Matik kacha arihava	:	An ideal daughter-in-law
Mayar kharara	:	Eldest son
Mayarnao	:	Boy/men
Mayarnao kashok	:	Masculinity
Meiphung	:	Literally, it means hearth, but in the kinship system, it refers to the sub-group of a clan; a lineage formed by group of families who are believed to be descendant of one father
Meisum	:	Time spend together by youths during their leisure time by the fireside
Mirai kakaza	:	According to the belief of the Tangkhuls, it may be defined as sadistic possession of a person by the spirit of another person

Nao khangalui	:	Hot water therapy for an infant
Naongalava	:	Daughter
Naongara	:	Children
Naoming kaphok	:	Name giving ceremony
Naoyan	:	Literally, it means 'seeing the baby'. It is a ritual of exposing the baby to outsider
Naoyansa	:	A ceremonial meat of the naoyan
Ngaha	:	Axe
Ngala kaphem	:	Sissy
Ngala khangakhot	:	Marriage
Ngalakhui khalui	:	Remarriage on the part of men
Ngalalong	:	Girl's dormitory
Ngalanao	:	Girl
Ngalanao kashok	:	Feminine
Ngalei kharar apam	:	Haunted places
Nganganao	:	Dolls
Ngaralui	:	Terraced fields
Ngasotnao	:	Peer group/ friend
Oja	:	Teacher
Paisho	:	Youngest
Paitu	:	Bag
Paiyansa	:	Declaration meat
Pam	:	Literally means seat; marriageable cousins
Pangthem	:	Handicraft
Phanit	:	Festival
Phanit phanao	:	Festivities
Phapkata	:	Understanding
Phukreila	:	Women who marry outside the village and play a role in settling dispute between two warring groups
Prohowui phakachizat	:	Lord's Supper
Ramnao	:	Co-villagers
Rayilui	:	Wet terraced fields
Samkok	:	A straight cut at the front till the eye-brows keeping a little longer at the sides to cover the ear and keep it long at the back (usually a woman's hair-cut before marriage)
Samra	:	Drained water from rice
Saothei	:	Flat but round seed extracted from a creeper's plant called Saorong in local parlance
Saorong	:	A creeper plant

Sashitsa	: A piece of meat received as the symbol of entering the probationary period to the longshim
Sayur	: Animals (toy animal in the context)
Seluthi	: Small marbles made out of clay which they use for catapult
Shakaza	: Wedding
Shaksakhami	: A kind of bride presentation where women are presented with different items at the time of her marriage by her parents and kin members
Shanao	: Women
Shang akhavaiva	: Wife of the clan's head
Shang akhava	: Clan head
Shangnao	: Clan
Shar	: Genna
Sharwo	: Priest
Sheba sakathei	: Caring
Shim akhavaiva	: Wife of the householder
Shimlam	: Presents and gifts to a bride
Shimluikat	: Legally authorised person who inherits the property
Shimkhur	: Family
Shimkhur chinaongara	: Family members
Shimshar	: Household genna
Shimthui luithui khamiya	: Priest who performed the ritual marking the beginning of sowing and plantation
Shimva	: Householder
Shitkasangrin	: Religion
Shokhala	: Literally, it means upside-down; refers to violation of clan exogamy
Silui	: Mithun
Sop	: Carrying basket
Tang	: Locality/khel
Tangkhul Long	: The Tangkhul Tribal council
Tarong	: A platform built alongside the hut
Thangthang	: Toy kitchenware
Tharshat	: Festival for bountiful harvest and prosperous life
Theithukthei	: Wild apples
Thingkari	: Cycle made of wood
Thisham	: Death Anniversary
Vahem	: Ceremony of acknowledging the marriage of couples who elope

Vakhalat	:	A kind of incest which means coming back to the maternal uncle
Varei	:	Maternal uncle
Veishir	:	Ceremony of closing the village gate
Yarra	:	Festival of the youth
Yarthot	:	Labour groups on the basis of age gratings that perform cultivation works in rotation
Yorla	:	Married sisters and daughters
Yotpak	:	Spade
Zatkang	:	Burnt rice
Zavar	:	The last ceremony marking the end of Chumphu

Bibliography

Aier, Anungla. 2008. 'Folklore, Folk Ideas and Gender Among the Nagas'. In *Eastern Quarterly: Gender Studies in North-East.* pp. 87-93, Vol. 5, Issues II & III. Manipur Research Forum.

Ardener, E. 1972. 'Belief and the Problem of Women'. In *The Interpretation of Ritual.* J.S. La Fontaine (ed). London: Tavistock.

Barnard, A. and J. Spencer (eds). 1996. *Encyclopedia of Social and Cultural Anthropology.* London: Routledge.

Beauvoir, Simone de. 1972 (1949). *The Second Sex.* Harmondsworth: Penguin Books Ltd.

Behera, Deepak Kumar and Namita Nanda. 1997. 'Gender Inequality in a Tribal Context: Some Reflections from Orissa'. In Pfeffer, G and Behera, D. K. (eds), *Contemporary Society: Tribal Studies,* volume one. New Delhi: Concept Publishing Company.

Bell, Diane.1983. *Daughters of the Dreaming.* Melbourne: McPhee Gribble.

Benhabib, S. 1992. *Situating the Self: Gender, Community, and Post-Modernism in Contemporary Ethics.* London: Routledge.

Bhandari, Sudhanshu. 2010. 'Prostitution in Colonial India'. In *Mainstream,* Vol. XLVIII, No. 26. Gale: Al Bawaba (Middle East) Ltd.

Bodgan, Robert and Stevens J. Taylor. 1975. *Introduction to Qualitative Research Methods: A Phenomenological Approach to Social Sciences.* New York: A Wiley- Interscience Publication.

Brown, P. and L. Jordanova. 1982. 'Oppressive Dichotomies: The Nature/Culture Debate'. In *Women in Society: Interdisciplinary Essays.* Cambridge Women's Studies Group (ed). pp. 224-221. London: Virago.

Butler, Judith. 1990. *Gender Trouble: Feminism and the Subversion of Identity.* New York: Routledge.

Chandra, Sudhir (ed). 2008. *Enslaved Daughters: Colonialism, Law, and Women's Rights.* Second Edition. Oxford: Oxford University Press.

Connell, R. W. 2002. *Gender.* Cambridge: Polity Press.

Croll, Elizabeth. 2000. *Endangered Daughters: Discrimination and Development in Asia.* London: Routledge.

Dube, Leela. 1997. *Women and Kinship: Comparative Perspective on Gender in South and South-East Asia.* New Delhi: Vistaar Publications.

Dube, Leela. 2009. *Women and Kinship*. New Delhi: Rawat Publications.

Faithorn, Elizabeth. 1976. 'Women as Persons: Aspects of Female Life and Male-Female Relationships Among the Kafe'. In *Man amd Women in the New Guinea Highlands.* P. Brown and G. Buchbinder (eds). *American Anthropological Association*, Special Publication, No. 8.

Furer-Haimendorf, C. Von. 1933. *The Naked Nagas.* Calcutta: Thacker Spink and Co.

Gangoli, Geetanjali. 2007. 'Immortality, Hurt or Choice: Indian Feminist and Prostitution'. In *International Feminist Journal of Politics,* 9 (1). London: Routledge.

Gillison, Gillian. 1980. 'Images of Nature in Gimi Thought'. In MacCormack and M. Strathern eds, *Nature, Culture and Gender,* Cambridge: Cambridge University Press.

______ 1993. *Between Culture and Fantasy: A New Guinea Highlands Mythology.* London: University of Chicago Press.

Goodale, Jane. 1980. 'Gender, Sexuality and Marriage: A Kaulong Model of Nature and Culture'. In *Nature, Culture and Gender.* MacCormack and M. Strathern (eds). Cambridge: Cambridge University Press.

Haq, Ihsanul. 2007. 'Patriarchal Ideology and Gender Imbalance in India'. In *Eastern Anthropologist,* Vol. 60, No. 2. New Delhi: Serial Publications.

Harris, M. 1993. *Culture, People, Nature.* Sixth edition. New York: Harper Collins College Publishers.

Herskovits, Melville J. 1948. *Man and His Works.* New York: Alfred a Knopt Publisher.

______ 1955. *Cultural Anthropology: An Abridged Revision of Man and His Works.* New Delhi: Oxford and IBH Publishing Co.

History of Somdal Baptist Church, Centenary Publication. 2009.

Hodson, T. C. 1911. *The Naga Tribes of Manipur.* London: MacMillan and Co., Ltd.

Holden, L. 2008. *Hindu Divorce: A Legal Anthropology*. Hampshire: Ashgate Publishing Ltd.

Horam, M. 1977. *Social and Cultural Life of the Nagas*. New Delhi: B. R. Publishing Corporation.

______ 1988. *Nagas Old Ways and New Trends.* New Delhi: Cosmo Publications.

Hutton, J. H. 1930. 'Head Hunting.' In *Man in India.* Vol. V.

Indira, R and Shanthi. 1997. 'Gender Dynamics in the Context of a Tribal Society: The Case of Jenukurubas'. In Pfeffer, G and Behera, D. K. (eds). *Contemporary Society: Tribal Studies,* Volume one. New Delhi: Concept Publishing Company.

Jordanova, L. 1980. 'Natural Facts: A Historical Perspective on Science and Sexuality'. In *Nature, Culture and Gender.* C. P. MacCormack and M. Strathern (eds). pp. 42-69. Cambridge: Cambridge University Press.

Khare, R. S. 1992. 'From Kanya to Mata: Aspects of the Cultural Language of Kinship in Northern India'. In *Concepts of persons: Kinship, Caste, and Marriage in India.* Akos Ostor, Lina Fruzz Etti, and Steve Barnett (eds). Delhi: Oxford University Press.

Leacock, Eleanor. 1978. 'Women's Status in Egalitarian Society: Implications for Social Evolution'. *Current Anthropology*. 19 (2): 247-275.

Lewin, Ellen. 2006. *Feminist Anthropology: A Reader.* Oxford: Blackwell Publishing Ltd.

Lorber, Judith Moore Jean Lisa. 2007. *Gendered Bodies: Feminist Perspectives.* California: Roxbury Publishing Company.

Luikham, R. 2009. *Tangkhul Traditional Land Use System and Related Custom.* Ukhrul: Ukhrul District Community Resource Management Society.

Madan, T. N. 1992. 'The Ideology of the Householder among the Kashmiri Pandits'. In *Concepts of Persons: Kinship, Caste, and Marriage in India.* Akos Ostor, Lina Fruzz Etti, and Steve Barnett (ed). Delhi: Oxford University Press.

Major, Andrea (ed). 2006. *Sati: A Historical Anthology*. Oxford: Oxford University Press.

Malinowski, Bronislaw. 1927. *Sex and Repression in Savage Society.* London: Routledge and Kegan Paul.

Mead, M. 1935. *Sex and Temperament in Three Primitive Societies*. New York: Morrow.

Meillasoux, Claude. 1981. *Maidens, Meal and Money.* Cambridge: Cambridge University Press.

Mills, J. P. 1935. 'The Head - Hunters of Assam.' In *Royal Central Asian Journal.* Vol. XXII, pp. 418-24.

Moore, Henrietta L. 1986. *Space, text and Gender: An Anthropological Study of the Marakwet of Kenya.* Cambridge: Cambridge University Press.

______ 1988. *Feminism and Anthropology.* Cambridge: Polity Press.

______ 1994. *A Passion for Difference: Essays in Anthropology and Gender.* Bloomington, Indiana: Indiana University Press.

______ 2007. *The subject of Anthropology: Gender Symbolism and Psychoanalysis.* Cambridge: Polity Press.

Mukhim, Patricia. 2009. 'Khasi Matrilineal Society'. In *Societies of Peace: Matriarchies Past, Present and Future.* Goettner-Abendroth Heidi (ed). Toronto: Inanna Publications and Education Inc.

Nongbri, Tiplut. 1996. 'Problems of Matriliny: A Short Review on the Khasi Kinship Structure'. In *Kinship and Family in North East.* J. S. Bhandari (ed). Vol. 2, 329-345. New Delhi: Cosmo Publications.

______ 2008. 'Deconstructing Musculinity: Fatherhood, Matriliny and Social Change'. In *Eastern Quarterly: Gender Studies in North-East.* pp. 75-86, Vol. 5, Issues II & III. Manipur Research Forum.

Ortner, Sherry. 1974. 'Is Female to Male as Nature is to Culture?'. In *Woman, Culture and Society*. M. Rosaldo and M. Lamphere (eds). pp. 67-88. Stanford: Stanford University Press.

Ortner, S and H. Whitehead (eds). 1981. *Sexual Meanings.* pp. 166-91. Cambridge: Cambridge University Press.

Overing, J. 1996. 'Aesthetic in a Cross- Cultural Category: Against the Motion'. In *Key Debates in Anthropological Theory*. Tim Ingald (ed). pp. 276-293. London: Routledge.

Pakyntien, V. 1999. 'Gender Preference in Khasi Society'. In *Wonder That is Culture*. T. B. Subba (ed). New Delhi: Mittal Publications.

Parsons, T. and R. Bales. 1956. *Family, Socialisation and Interaction Process*. London: Routledge.

Ramamurthy, P. 1994. 'Patriarchy and the Process of Agricultural Intensification in South India'. In *Gender and Political Economy: Explorations of South Asian Systems*. Alice W. Clark (ed). Delhi: Oxford University Press.

Rao, Nitya. 2008. *Good Women Do Not Inherit Land: Politics of Land and Gender in India*. New Delhi: Orient Blackswan Pvt. Ltd.

Rapport, N. and J. Overing. 2000. *Social and Cultural Anthropology: The Key Concepts*. London: Routledge.

Reddy, Gayatri. 2005. 'With Respect to Sex: Negotiating Hijra Identity in South India'. In *Worlds of Desire: The Chicago Series on Sexuality, Gender, and Culture*. Chicago: University of Chicago Press.

Reiter, R. R. 1975. 'Introduction'. In *Toward an Anthropology of Women*. R. R. Reiter (ed). pp. 11-19. New York: Monthly Review Press.

Rohni, Sahni, V. Kalyan Shankar and Hemant Apte (eds). 2008. *Prostitution and Beyond: An Analysis of Sex Work in India*. California: Sage Publications.

Rosaldo, M.Z. 1974. 'Women, Culture and Society: A Theoretical Overview'. In *Women, Culture and Society*. M. Z. Rosaldo and L. Lamphere (eds) Stanford: Stanford University Press.

Rosaldo, M. Z. and L. Lamphere (eds) *Women, Culture and Society*. Stanford: Stanford University Press.

Rubin, Gayle. 1975. The Traffic in Women: Notes on the Political Economy of Sex. In *Towards an Anthropology of Women*. R. R. Reiter (ed). pp. 157-210. New York: Monthly Review Press.

Rudolph, I. Lloyd and Susanne Hoeber. 1984. *The Modernity of Tradition: Political Development in India*. Chicago: The University of Chicago Press.

Ruivah, Khashim. 1993. *Social Changes among the Nagas (Tangkhul)*. New Delhi: Cosmo Publications.

Ruivah, Khashim and K. S. Ambrose Lurstep. 1996. 'Clan Organisation and Kinship System of the Tangkhuls'. In *Kinship and Family in North East*. J. S. Bhandari (ed). Vol. 2, 329- 345. New Delhi: Cosmo Publications.

Sack, K. 1974. 'Engels Revisited: Women, the Organisation of Production, and Private Property'. In *Women, Culture and Society*. M. Z. Rosaldo and Louise Lamphere (eds). Stanford: Stanford University Press.

Schnieder, D. M. 1968. *American Kinship: A Cultural Account*. Eaglewood Cliffs, New Jersey: Prentice-Hall.

Sen, Sipra. 1992. *Tribes and Castes of Manipur*. New Delhi: Mittal Publications.

Sharma, Miriam and Urmila Vanjani. 1994. 'Engendering Reproduction: The Political Economy of Reproductive Activities in a Rajasthan Village'. In *Gender and Political Economy: Exploration of South Asian Systems.* Alice W. Clark (ed). pp. 24-65. Delhi: Oxford University Press.

Shimray, A. S. W. 2001. *History of the Tangkhul Nagas.* New Delhi: Akansha Publishing House.

Singh, Reena. 2001. *Gender Composition: Values, Preferences and Behavior.* New Delhi: Rawat Publications.

Stack, C. 1974. *All Our Kin: Strategies for Survival in a Black Community.* New York: Harper and Row.

Strathern, M. 1981. 'Self-interest and the Social Good: Some Implications in the Hagen Gender Imagery'. In *Sexual Meanings.* S. Ortner and H. Whitehead (eds). pp. 166-91. Cambridge: Cambridge University Press.

______ 1992. 'Parts and Wholes: Refiguring Relationships in a Post-plural World'. In *Conceptualising Society.* A. Kuper (ed). London: Routledge.

Viswewaran, Kamala. 1994. *Fictions of Feminist Ethnography.* Minneapolis: University of Minnesota Press.

______ 2004. 'Introduction- Engendering Violence: Boundaries, Histories and the Everyday'. *Cultural Dynamics* (Special Issues on *'Gender Violence in South Asia: Nation and Community in the Post colonial Present'*). Vol. 16 (2/3), pp. 125-39.

Weiner, A. 1976. *Women of Value, Men of Renown.* Austin: University of Texas Press.

Wharton, Amy S. 2005. *The Sociology of Gender: An Introduction to Theory and Research.* Oxford: Blackwell Publishing Ltd.

Yanagisako, Sylvia and Carol Delancy. 1995. *Naturalizing Power: Essays in Feminist Cultural Analysis.* New York: Routledge.

Young, Iris Marion. 2002. 'Lived body versus Gender: Reflections on Social Structure and Subjectivity'. In *Ratio,* Vol. 15, No. 4, pp. 410-428 (19). Oxford: Blackwell Publishing Ltd.

Zehol, L. 1998. *Women in Naga Society.* New Delhi: Regency Publications.

______ 2006. 'Gender Issues in the Tribal Society of the North-East: Some Observations.' In *Bulletin of the Department of Anthropology.* pp. 99-106, Vol. 34. Dibrugarh University.

Index

L

M

N

R

S

T